Come Again to the Circle

Come Again to the Circle

40 Leaders Imagine
the Church beyond COVID

WILLIAM B. KINCAID

WIPF & STOCK · Eugene, Oregon

COME AGAIN TO THE CIRCLE
40 Leaders Imagine the Church beyond COVID

Wipf & Stock
An Imprint of Wipf and Stock Publishers
199 W. 8th Ave., Suite 3
Eugene, OR 97401

www.wipfandstock.com

PAPERBACK ISBN: 978-1-6667-4956-4
HARDCOVER ISBN: 978-1-6667-4957-1
EBOOK ISBN: 978-1-6667-4958-8

VERSION NUMBER 110122

Unless otherwise noted, scripture quotation are from the New Revised
Standard Version Bible, copyright 1989, Division of Christian Education
of the National Council of the Churches of Christ in the United States of
America. Used by permission. All rights reserved.

Scripture quotations marked MSG are taken from *THE MESSAGE*, copy-
right © 1993, 1994, 1995, 1996, 2000, 2001, 2002 by Eugene H. Peterson.
Used by permission of NavPress. All rights reserved. Represented by
Tyndale House Publishers, Inc.

"The church is an invitation to come again to the circle,
to bring all of yourself,
to see and listen to one another and the meaning we share,
to discover who we are in that circle,
and then to come again and again,
each time with more to offer and each time learning more."

—Rev. Shannon Dycus

Contents

Acknowledgements

I AM DEEPLY GRATEFUL to everyone I talked with as part of this project. Whether we talked informally or in a structured interview, one-on-one or part of a group, briefly or in depth, all of you shared generously and insightfully. I thank you and I remain humbled by your willingness to participate in this research project at a time of such unrelenting uncertainty. I hope I have brought forward your voice, energy, wisdom, and commitment in ways that capture you and your ministry.

I directly quote several of the forty interviewees in this book. In other cases, I draw more generally from people's comments and reflections and appropriately reference those. What is important for you to know is that every interviewee contributed significantly to this project, even if not directly referenced. The collective wisdom of this experience formed the soundtrack for my writing.

I express my deep gratitude to the Trustees, Administration and Faculty Colleagues at Christian Theological Seminary in Indianapolis. A generous research leave policy made the undertaking of this project possible.

And finally, I thank the members and staff of First Christian Church in Frankfort, Kentucky, for the opportunity to serve as their Interim Senior Minister during a part of this study leave. My time with this historic congregation placed me in concrete situations, challenges and opportunities that prompted clearer and deeper reflection on what it feels like to be, as so many congregations are, at a rather significant crossroads of congregational life.

Acknowledgements

The people at First Christian Church, Frankfort, have been amazingly warm, appreciative and supportive and I am most grateful for the experience.

...duction

> ...ning, like Isaiah says, but the question is not just
> ...ceive it. The question is whether we will join in."
>
> —Rev. Christy Jo Harber

THAT WE live in a remarkable time hardly captures where
...e as individuals, as a country, and as the church. It does not
...en feel like a single time, but parallel dimensions of time that
obviously are related to one another and yet maintain their own
realities. The emotional highs and lows have stretched us during
this time, prompting notable imagination and innovation, while at
the same time inflicting grief and trauma in degrees that will take
considerable time from which to heal.

In the church, some pastors and congregations are fiercely
attempting to pick up where they left off, believing that the CO-
VID-19 pandemic created a pause from which they can return to
things as they were. We might wish that was the case, but that past
no longer exists. We might wish we could return to the perceived
safety of the will familiar, but the resurrected Christ has gone ahead
to Galilee and beckons us from there to participate in a new future.
That future will be informed by our past, but that past cannot be
recreated. And besides, lest nostalgia paralyzes us, was our recent
past our most animated life and faithful expression as Christians?

Other pastors and congregations know that the pandemic
did not so much cause change as highlight change that was well

1

underway. Many c
those changes. Still o
change around the con
the congregation. They a
back to revive what once wa
into the future either. Instead,
situation into something palata
too much of us, something that sto
hard conversations and concrete co
eloquently and passionately about injustic
they probably will not sign up for a cause or
In the broader community, as Rev. Wes
son said, "The virus gave our society a CT Scan
sibly deny what's here. There are signs of crisis every
Jim Sichko, pointing to the deep mistrust and danger
realities currently afoot in the U.S. was even more con
world is in an extremely angry mood."
COVID-19 pulled the curtain back. It exposed systemic i
uities and a level of anger that many had safeguarded themselve
from seeing and understanding. For many, especially among those
who in our privilege and comfort hung the curtain to begin with,
a craving surfaced to close the curtain and to return to life as we
thought of it before. As Rev. William Smith put it, "I knew the
system was broken, I just didn't know how badly broken it was."
The experience of Smith becoming infected with COVID-19 shed
further light on the barriers he and members of his congregation
faced at the intersection of race and healthcare.

We have experienced creativity and disruption, isolation and
fresh togetherness, new opportunities and intense grief, newfound
confidence and shattered assumptions. In all the dramatic swings,
what have we learned about ourselves, our faith and the church
during the several waves of the COVID-19 virus? What do we
now understand in undeniable terms about the gross and harsh
inequities that so many individuals and communities face? And
how has the experience of a pandemic sharpened and energized
the church's work in the world?

What difference will all of this make? Will the American church examine its identity, understand its practices, and connect its mission to the world that actually exists today? Will we become more involved in creating communities where all of God's children can flourish with dignity, safety and opportunity? Will our congregations reprioritize and reallocate our time, energy and resources to address the gaps and injustices around us?

Or, will the learning of the last two and a half years be for naught as we frantically crave a return to life before March 2020?

These are not new questions or exercises for us, but neither are they discussions that we have consistently ventured into with much openness and energy, nor sustained with much imagination. But things are different now. A tragic virus has presented us with an opportunity. It broke open conversations and held the light up to systems and situations that cry out for healing words and hopeful engagement. The questions may sound familiar, but the timing and circumstances are creating another moment for us to hear and respond to them differently.

This book focuses on the church transcending COVID, on being the church beyond COVID rather than a church defined by it. This is not a book about COVID-19! Nor is it an exhaustive and exhausting post-mortem.

This book focuses on leveraging the learning from this awful pandemic for the sake of the world God desires. It's a resource for you in considering and acting on questions like these. I wrote it to aid congregations like yours to understand and claim some of the opportunities and challenges you have faced and will face. I wanted to connect imaginative and engaged individuals and congregations with those of you who are working as catalysts for change in your own churches and communities.

This book seeks to leverage the experiences and learnings from the pandemic for a new season of fruitful ministry. For our learning to translate into action and for the church to be a credible, relevant witness to the gospel, conversations that broke open during the pandemic must remain open. Otherwise, we will have wasted these opportunities, drifted again from our spiritual foundations and identity, and turned away from the pain, violence and marginalization that diminishes and, in many cases, destroys human life.

Forty

In the Fall of 2021, in the midst of the Delta variant, I interviewed forty faith leaders from around the country to understand how they were living into the question, "What matters now?" It was an amazingly fulfilling experience. I loved hearing how so many of them are "oddly energized," as one interviewee put it, even while facing daunting uncertainty. The interviews repeatedly brought sobering moments of tragedy and loss, as well as surprising congregational initiatives and flexibility.

I was surprised by the energy and hopefulness that people brought to these interviews. Admittedly, I selected the interviewees, either through prior connections with them or through the recommendations of others. I could skew the pool of interviewees toward the energetic and discerning and I probably did. Obviously, I wanted to talk with people who were looking ahead with anticipation and able to reflect hopefully on the question "What matters now?" In the midst of loss and chaos, so many of them are looking forward to the next season of ministry and congregational life. This is particularly true of those who believe they now have the chance to reset their ministry and to help craft something fresh and relevant within their congregation. For them, this resetting is a welcomed and unexpected opportunity.

I began this research expecting to hear a frequent and strong emphasis on the church's activism in the world, especially as it relates to racial inequity. Nearly everyone named understanding the realities and implications of race in America as a priority. A few focused on racial equity during major portions of the hour-long interview. Most hoped that a spiral of learning and advocacy was developing in light of the then-recent, tragic and avoidable deaths of George Floyd and Breonna Taylor. That spiral would bring together prayerful reflection and protest, each one learning from and deepening the other.

Most interviewees expressed similar concerns about the economic challenges, the diminishing rights of women, the hostilities toward members of the LGBTQ community, and the indifference toward environmental degradation. A few interviewees articulated intersectional concerns that highlighted the particular challenges, for instance, of African-American women in church communities or the economic challenges facing many Trans people.

These constitute obviously important and urgent concerns, but even the overwhelming number of interviewees who raised these issues named something else as the starting point. Numerous pastors spoke of reprioritizing their ministry to emphasize spiritual practices, the fostering of Christian community, the equipping of congregants for grassroots involvement in the world, and an approach to pastoral care that understands the immediate and lasting effects of trauma. Again, these priorities all sound like things at the center of pastoral work, but the pandemic confronted pastors and other congregational leaders with time-consuming preoccupations that may keep church people busy and happy, but have little to do with the vocational core of ministry and the mission of the church.

Nearly everyone expressed some level of regret about previously allocating insufficient time to nurture a vibrant Christian identity in the congregation, to teach more intentionally about major biblical themes and to engage especially in discernment and theological reflection. On a related note, most interviewees also lamented how little energy they gave prior to the pandemic on fostering a congregational identity centered in the life of Jesus. Many expressed the hope that the church would overcome its propensity and excuses for distraction and commit to a serious and sustained focus on being a transforming presence in the world. In other words, let's focus on being the church. That phrase means different things to different people, but at the heart of that statement lies the need to better understand the commitments we make as followers

COME AGAIN TO THE CIRCLE

of Jesus in today's world and cultivating the spiritual depth to enact those commitments.

Thanks to Zoom, I interviewed people from Queens to Miami, Florida, all through the Midwest, Mid-South and Southwest, and on to the West Coast. Some interviewees live in consistently "blue" parts of the country, while others can be found in deeply "red" areas. For example, at the time of her interview, Rev. Aqueelah Ligonde served a Presbyterian congregation in Queens, New York. Congresswoman Grace Meng, an ally of Speaker Nancy Pelosi, represents that district in the U.S. House. Rev. Hugh Hendrickson, on the other hand, serves in a Georgia town represented in the U.S. House by Andrew Clyde, a local gun dealer and decorated Navy commander who voted against certifying the 2020 presidential election results. Context matters and these interviews reflect that.

Very few of these forty interviewees serve in congregations and communities flush with resources and obvious options. Most of them scramble about for resources for ongoing ministry, deal with serious and seemingly never-ending questions about the church building, and serve congregations with dwindling influence. Some of the congregations are growing in participation. Others are stable or declining. At least three of the interviewees actually planted brand new congregations during the pandemic!

The group of interviewees is racially and generationally diverse. Women comprise a slight majority. Interviewees come from historic Protestant denominations, Progressive Evangelical circles and both Catholic and Orthodox traditions. The forty interviewees have a wide range of pastoral experience and come from various seasons of ministry—early, mid, and late career. The ministry settings are fairly evenly distributed among small towns, midsized towns, urban and suburban areas. Eight of the forty serve the church through leadership in denominational, academic and organizational settings. Those who are pastors serve in congregations of various sizes.

This diverse group of leaders represents amazing depth and conviction. Their comments are powerful and their courage is unmistakable. They are not waiting for a post-COVID timeframe to assess and engage the situation. They refuse to wait until everything falls apart and then try to pick up the pieces. They also refuse to allow the issues that rose to undeniable recognition during this pandemic to disappear from the radar of our public life and the church's mission.

Just as we have witnessed courageous acts from those on the front lines of healthcare, public services and education, these leaders demonstrate daring and inspiring examples of faithfulness, experimentation, innovation, expanded ministries and surging clarity about the church's vocation and commitments. They know too well that individuals and systems alike crave comfort and can quickly snap back into the safe and the familiar apart from the ongoing, intentional discernment of what God is inviting us to consider.

In the midst of disruption, they created space for timely and perceptive conversations, which led to startling yet freeing honesty about the denial and defaults that were operating in those situations. Those conversations often continued beyond the diagnosis stage where congregations so regularly stall and into bold and rather speedy decision-making processes, all in the midst of a pandemic.

The distillation of wisdom and courage from these interviews will both inform and inspire. This book allows you to listen to and consider for yourselves key themes and opportunities by which to express our faith, whether that faith involves tenderness or rage or both. In these pages, you hear from pastoral leaders who are stepping into what has broken open. They are demanding by their integrity to the gospel that we take note of what we see and hear and judge it against what God desires for the world. They are offering courageous, faithful and imaginative ways forward, not the least of which is their persistence in holding before us oppressive, exclusive situations that cannot stand.

These leaders and their congregations and organizations are keeping the learnings of these last few years before us. While continuing to care for and stand with individuals and communities in peril, they also are refreshing and infusing the larger questions of church with urgency and significance. This is a time to take advantage of everything being on the table. It's a time to reconsider the gospel and think afresh about the practices of our faith. It's a time to give a candid appraisal of where we are as a church, to make an honest assessment of what impact we really have, to engage with more focus and urgency, and to recover what is at the core of being followers of Jesus.

The stories and wisdom shared here are important for our remembering and our grieving. They are equally critical in focusing our ministry, inspiring our participation and sustaining our action. The fierce way these leaders are pursuing issues and questions will cause others to recognize the possibilities of this moment and to engage in ministry that is imaginative and liberative.

Numbers matter, especially in Scripture. Forty is one of those numbers.

I want to claim that the significance of the number forty emerged early from somewhere deep within my theological consciousness, but I confess, I did not initiate this research with the Bible's math in mind.

Instead, recognizing the desire and need to paint as complete a picture as possible, I developed a list of potential interviewees that not only would represent diverse perspectives, contexts and ministry experiences, but also would provide diversity within each category. For example, I knew the value of hearing and featuring Millennial voices in this research. At the same time, I wanted to capture the diversity of ministry settings, experiences and dreams among the millennials that I interviewed, so I interviewed several pastors and leaders from that age group in order to understand and portray well that diversity. Forty became the number of interviewees needed in order to accomplish the goals of this project.

But somewhere along the way, I realized that forty was exactly the number. We were and are in a wilderness time and the anxiety and grief of the wilderness will not be solved by returning to Egypt. At the end of each interview, I asked "What image or story or theme is helping you make sense of this time?" Over a fourth of the interviewees named the Israelites wandering in the wilderness as the defining image, though interestingly, not everyone named the same features of that wilderness time. Some highlighted the need to understand the in-between nature of this time. Others pointed to Moses' leadership. Still others shared reflections on daily manna and so on.

In addition to the forty formal interviews, I also want to give thanks for two conversations, each with seven participants, that helped to confirm this as a timely project and to help think through interview possibilities. Also, I surveyed twenty participants in First Season Project and met with twenty more through a conversation with Launchpad Partners. I am grateful to each person.

One way the diversity of this list reveals itself is through titles. For example, while most are ordained ministers, some are not. Some serve in traditions that do not ordain persons or assign them the title of reverend. I am sensitive to the fact that titles, credentials and degrees get recognized differently in different communities and traditions. They sometimes reveal privilege. When they go unacknowledged, we perpetuate exclusive systems and do further harm. For that reason, I asked each interviewee how they would like their name to appear at the end of this book. The diversity of interviewees accounts for the many ways the names are listed.

How Your Congregation Can Use This Book

The American church will outlast the COVID-19 virus. Even in the likely event of the virus becoming endemic, most American congregations will survive for the immediate future. We can be fairly confident of this. Let's embrace that piece of good news, but let's acknowledge two realities.

First, a much higher number of congregations will close as a result of COVID than normally would in a year's time and a greater percentage of congregations that remain open will slip closer toward concluding their ministry and closing their doors. In some cases, that conclusion may be a decade or more away. In other situations, the slip feels sooner and more drastic than that.

Second, nearly every congregation will be smaller going forward; in some cases, significantly smaller. This will bring into play an array of interesting and startling questions. It may lead to greater intentionality for the church's focus. Or, it may exacerbate the grief and the urge to attempt a return to what was, even if what was never really was.

What we can be far less confident about is whether the church will ever fully live beyond the virus's definition and limitations. The question of "What will characterize the life and the witness of the church going forward?" will depend on the active discernment, courageous temperament and creative engagement of pastors and congregants alike. As you read what these leaders share, note that they do not prescribe a singular path for all pastors and congregations. What you will find here are numerous points of resonance, connection and starting points for your particular context.

The book raises themes and circumstances from diverse contexts that will allow you to customize actionable commitments for your context. It is about next steps. It is about action. Congregations will pursue opportunities and issues differently due to a variety of traditions, callings, contexts and circumstances, but in the end, these stories and situations are only honored by joining in that pursuit, by making an investment ourselves. This book is about engagement—your engagement and mine. As Rev. Christy Jo Harber put it, the question is whether we will join the new thing God is doing.

You might use this book in one of two ways. First, it can serve as a resource for your leadership council or team, a group that is probably already accustomed to thinking through scenarios, opportunities and challenges. In that case, you will engage this book in a familiar manner and the reflections and priorities will spill out from the leadership group into the congregation. On one hand, people will find this approach comfortable. On the other hand, this approach probably will not yield the kind of broad conversation and creative activity needed in this time.

The second way to use this book is to create small groups comprised of people who generally do not connect with each other in the congregation. They may know each other, but their interests or backgrounds or time spent in the congregation do not bring them together very often. This arrangement will allow for exciting, challenging, fruitful conversations as a result of the differing and diverse perspectives represented.

For this second approach, here is a six-step process for using this book.

1. Seek a congregational commitment to study this book, including an endorsement by your congregation's governing body (board, council, deacons, etc.)

2. Form at least one and, if possible, additional diverse groups of six to eight persons (depending on the size of your congregation) and identify who the convenor of each group will be. Rather than draw on existing groups, such as the elders or choir or women's group, bring people together into each group who are not usually grouped together. Attempt to create groups that include diverse theological, social and political views. Use this process to get know people in your congregation better and to bring different perspectives into conversation with each other.

3. Read and discuss the book over a six-month period, reading a chapter before each gathering and being prepared to discuss that chapter at the meeting. For the first session, read the Introduction and Chapter One. Each chapter includes a list of five questions for discussion. Many of these questions come from the interviewees for this project.

4. Invite me, the author, to join each small group at least once (bkincaid@cts.edu) to help facilitate the conversation and so that I can continue my own learning from you.

5. Plan a congregation-wide gathering at the end of the six-month period as a time for groups to share with others your congregation's key issues and opportunities.

6. Encourage your congregation's governing body, along with the pastor, to commit to specific, impactful and time-bound steps to engage three to five of those key issues and opportunities.

Perhaps when this book is in print the waves of COVID-19 will have eased and we will be finding our footing. Still, there likely will not truly be a post-COVID time. In light of that, we listen for what God is inviting us to consider. Once discerned, in what ways will we step beyond our usual patterns in order to participate? What will receive our devotion, energy and openness? And what will we absolutely stop doing because it takes energy and focus away from our core values and commitments?

My hope is that this book will be the impetus to come again to the circle, to gather your congregational leaders into a prayerful and intentional season of discernment, "to come together honestly," as one of the interviewees put it, to ask "what matters now?" and then to act on what you discern. This has always been the question of the church. Now it's our time to answer.

One

"The church is an invitation to come again to the circle,
to bring all of yourself,
to see and listen to one another and the meaning we share,
to discover who we are in that circle,
and then to come again and again,
each time with more to offer and each time learning more."

—REV. SHANNON DYCUS

THE RESPONSES BY REV. Shannon Dycus to the question of what matters now brought into the foreground the importance of understanding first who we are as the church and what the experience of the church can be. Dycus serves as Dean of Students at Eastern Mennonite University. Her ministry includes significant congregational leadership as well. Dycus's statement would have stayed with me anyway for its truth, but I also trust it because I know it grows out of experience and investment in the Christian community.

"Come again to the circle," Dycus said. That is the invitation of the church, especially now. Congregations find various ways to make that invitation. Now, though, many hear "come again to the circle" as the invitation of a church that is irrelevant, distrustful, self-serving and in crisis. We make that invitation harder to hear and trust when we turn away from the world and kick into our full self-preservation mode. People can sense the ways that the invitation is tainted by a congregational obsession over survival. We cloud the invitation further when we do not name and engage what is happening before our very eyes and instead double our efforts to return things to exactly as they were in whatever era most benefits us.

The rush back to another, albeit vague and unspecified time will generate such a thick nostalgia that the more discerning recipients of this invitation will shake their heads at the lack of connection and integration to life and questions of the current moment. An invitation to the circle enshrined with this temperament will not be experienced as authentic, resonant or relevant.

There is no question that how congregations entered the pandemic went a long way toward how they would move through it. Some congregations, even in their fatigue and anxiety, laid the groundwork for daring moves over the last few years. They navigated a life-altering virus, the ensuing shutdowns, and the many shifts and adjustments. They were already dealing with their own challenges, some of them very serious ones, but the pandemic seemed to frame their situation for them in clearer ways, as if it awakened them to life at the crossroads of their past and future. They recognized and practiced their adaptability, pursuing organizational learning, engaging in anti-racism causes, protests and studies, and rediscovering their individual and collective identity and practices as followers of Jesus.

These congregations, however few and far flung on the religious landscape they may be, positioned themselves to make a genuine invitation to come again to the circle. And in doing so, they appear ready to make that phrase not just the invitation, but as Dycus describes it, the very experience of church—to bring all of ourselves, to enter into meaningful mutuality, to know again the depth of faith and the height of its joy, and to grow and find our way together.

"Come again to the circle" resounds with genuine gentleness and warmth, but it also reverberates with an orienting and empowering vision of life shaped in community with one another. For example, most people seemed to miss being together for worship and fellowship during the pandemic, but our physical separation from each other revealed deeper issues, namely that most congregations had not focused on cultivating an experience of community that sufficiently connected people or prepared us to live well and faithfully in the world. As Rev. Brian Derrer put it, "We discovered just how poorly we were doing some very basic things and how much we were asking of a single hour on Sunday morning."

"To discover who we are in that circle."

Here's the good news: it's not too late to come again to the circle! It's not too late "to become a community of deep spirituality, generous love and transforming action," as Rev. Dr. Dick Hamm put it. It's not too late to foster a brimming life in the circle that overflows into the world as compassion, justice and relevance.

Here are a few examples. At New Beginnings Fellowship Church, where Dr. Alexia Ellis serves as executive pastor, the pandemic caused the leadership to identify and respond to urgent areas of need. Ellis said, "I have never seen so many Black men cry. It's trauma on top of trauma on top of trauma." Interestingly, an unexpected partner emerged as the church began thinking about how to support people in their grief. An advance team from Verizon came to the church's neighborhood ahead of expanding its presence and menu of services on the east side of Indianapolis. The Verizon representatives talked about being good neighbors and working with local organizations.

When they mentioned the idea of a partnership, Ellis told them, "Here's what being a partner can look like. We need support to get our grief groups going. You can be a financial partner in this." The Verizon folks probably didn't expect an ask like that. They likely thought they could introduce themselves and leave without having to back up their talk of partnership, but before they left Ellis had secured a $15,000 grant that would underwrite an initial round of ministry efforts in the area of grief counseling and support. In this most recent of daring and discerning moves at New Beginnings, they invited hurting people to come again to the circle.

Woodland Christian Church, a Disciples of Christ congregation in Lexington, Kentucky, addressed the strain of maintaining a beautiful but under-used and deteriorating building by partnering with a local development company. The development company will be granted a long-term land lease giving them control and responsibility for maintaining the building, and Woodland will continue its life and witness from a cherished location in the heart of Lexington. The endeavor will also expand Woodland's ministry by providing the space for much-needed affordable housing for seniors. Rev. Christy Jo Harber, Woodland's pastor, celebrates this innovative partnership, but also places it in the larger context of focusing the congregation on being a welcoming, liberative community for its immediate neighborhood and the world. Woodland has positioned itself to invite people to come again to an ever-expanding circle by freeing itself from property concerns that threaten to distract from or stifle that invitation.

Dr. Theodis Johnson, who serves as pastor of Sweet Home Baptist Church in Miami, Florida, and several colleagues traveled the state of Florida to meet with White pastors, hoping to spark new and renewed engagement on the issue of race and systemic racism. This occurred in the context of the Department of Homeland Security during the Trump administration declaring White Supremacy as the most persistent and lethal threat in the U.S. And of course, these travels and meetings occurred in some of the most uncertain months of the pandemic.

In the midst of cries for justice, African American and White pastors talked with each other, committed to fellowship together, and participated in honest conversations about what they were experiencing and feeling during this time. It would have been more convenient and less costly for all of them to make some assumptions and post them on social media, as people are prone to do these days. It would have been far less tense and tiring to have never reached out in the first place and, in turn, for the White pastors to decline the invitation to meet and talk. But the church, remember, is an invitation to come again to the circle. The path will not magically appear before us, nor will it magically be made void of barriers and cost. Often times, we will need to create the path and to navigate the twists and turns if we are to see and listen to one another and discover who we are in that circle.

Derrer, who serves as pastor of Christ the Savior Lutheran Church (ELCA) in Fishers, Indiana, talked about disrupting the grind of life so we can be open to the Spirit's presence and leading. Three key priorities emerged for him during a recent sabbatical that comprise a compelling vision for life in the circle at Christ the Savior: a sense of belonging, spiritual practices and milestones. More important than whether these happen in-person or online, he noted the flexibility and persistence needed to weave these three commitments into the fabric of individual and congregational life. "These won't happen accidentally," Derrer said. Belonging and spiritual practices received frequent mentions in these interviews. His inclusion of milestones as a way to deepen faith and community stood out. He described their importance by saying, "These are life transitions where we name God's presence. It may be a child beginning college, a relationship beginning or ending, moving to a new home or a new job—we want to help people name God's presence all along their journeys." What a hopeful way for our participation in the circle to shape our life beyond the circle.

I cannot paint an exact picture of what the future of your congregation will or needs to look like, but many people now find themselves at the crossroads of deep hunger for meaning, on the one hand, and a massive evaluation of whether to continue with their church participation, on the other. The invitation that Dycus articulates rings true in the following ways.

First, the experience of church captured by Dycus's image of the circle offers a learning community equal to the hunger and seriousness people carry. A learning community, she says, is always following up on what is happening by asking new questions and, when it is appropriate to the gospel to do so, going in new directions. The surprising learning by the church over the last few years need not be initiated by or confined to a time of panic, uncertainty or disaster. It seems trite to offer this, but let's remember that the meaning of the word disciple is to learn. That happens individually, for sure, but churches that live well in every season continually learn as a congregation and as an organization. Their shared faith deepens and grows as much as their individual faith.

Second, to imagine the church as a circle is to begin breaking down the hierarchy that sets up some as the experts and everyone else as the subjects. When Rev. Jevon Caldwell-Gross imagines the church now and into the future, he says that experts aren't allowed, in part because we are in such a new moment that no one qualifies. He also warns against how established (and sometimes self-appointed!) experts, whether they be clergy or laity, can implement and continue such inflexible patterns that the church cannot meet new opportunities and challenges.

We are all leaders in some shape or form. Those who hold onto the expert-hierarchy and expert-authority model are failing us, Dycus argues, by creating a stifling culture of oppression and by situating some people outside the accountability structures. We may think of scandals and celebrities exploiting the benefits of the hierarchy, but that stifling culture develops in quieter, less noticed and controversy-free settings, but with the same suffocating insularity and gridlock as the outcome.

Third, life in the circle prepares us for life in the world. Dycus says, "We can't show up well in the world apart from growing together in community. We've made discipleship into a matter of individual formation, but how did the first twelve learn? Together. And how will we learn? Together!" The mutuality and growth inherent in this image also provide the best chance to nurture a faith that can transcend political division.

The challenge for us is that the church fosters as much individualism as the culture does. When we layer on political conflict and national division, as well as our collective aversion to exploring timely and important issues, we are left with a faith experience unable to come together and share life with much depth and authenticity. "How strongly and wrongly we have understood ourselves only as individuals and not part of a community," Dycus laments.

"What is the value-added of church?"

The invitation to come again to the circle comes at a time when people are asking the value-added question about what the church brings to their lives. The defaults about church participation have been deteriorating for some time and, in some cases, never existed. As several staff members at the Indianapolis Center for Congregations said, some traditions and rituals already had lost value. They did not translate to younger generations, so they were hanging by a thread before. Now it's pretty easy for them to just move on.

Several interviewees framed this reality with the timely question for this section: "What is the value-added of church?" This question gained far more explicit traction during the pandemic. Many had kept the habit of church-going over many years, then the habit was broken. Suddenly, people wondered why they kept that habit for so long. "Why do I do this?" they began to ask. People at that point, including some long-time churchgoers, had to make a choice to step back into church. And not only a choice, people needed a reason to do so.

The COVID-19 virus created a moment in which people surprised themselves with how comfortably they asked, "If I stay home, am I really missing anything?" Clearly, some desperately missed seeing each other in the same room at the same time. Some missed the physicality of worship and the greetings and hugs of other worshippers, but that does not hold true for everyone. The Rev. Julia Whitworth reminds us that not everybody craved togetherness during the shutdown, nor are many of them craving it now that in-person activities have resumed. Rev. Dr. Chantal McKinney offers another angle on this, citing it as an opportunity for people to extract themselves from a church-promoted busyness that fails to deliver spiritual nourishment or call people into any meaningful engagement with the world.

As in-person activities slowly resumed between surges of the virus in the fall of 2021, interviewees voiced a significant shift in what they were seeing. To that point, the rate at which people were returning to in-person participation was slow but steady. By November 2021, nearly ever interviewee made a comment like, "It's likely that those who are back in-person now comprise a majority of those who are coming back." A serious plateau developed at that point that created anxiety among those who could only imagine the post-pandemic church as being very much like the pre-pandemic one. As several interviewees put it, "The default no longer holds and people aren't coming back in the way we hoped and probably won't until we answer the value-added question."

Whether congregants are voicing it in exactly this way, variations on the value-added question remain. What does the church singularly provide? What will life in the circle bring to my life and what will life in the circle ask of me?

Let's note how important it is for everyone to ask that first question, including those who have happily and rather uncritically returned to in-person worship, and then consider what will be asked of us in exploring this question.

To the first question, the more people who answer the value-added question the better, both for themselves and for the church. It will lead to more meaningful participation in the circle, but we should not assume that those who have returned to in-person participation have sufficiently answered that question. They may not have even asked it. It's possible that the strength of their defaults about going to church override the obviousness of the question. They may be so steeped in institutional participation of various kinds that they will see their questioning as a kind of betrayal. Most of these people will be older, but not all. Among some young boomers and Gen Xers especially, we find outliers who value institutional life for a variety of emotional, family and civic reasons, even when the story and practices of faith do not resonate in any stirring way.

In short, we should not assume that people have resumed some form of church participation because they have articulated the value-added proposition. Conversations that explore this question will be rough sledding among unreflective people, but even a few who can name the value-added experience of church can serve as catalysts in their congregations for at least appreciating the question.

For those who have stepped back, some will realize that the church does not add value or energy or purpose to their lives. They may remain tangentially related to the congregation, especially if doing so meets a perceived family need or community status, but most will look for additional ways to undergird their lives with meaning and connection.

The real opportunity exists among those for whom this is a live and important question. They are asking, What will my participation in this congregation do for my life that nowhere else will do? Not only must we surround these people with care and resources that allow them to hold space open for this discernment, but those who honestly pursue this question and arrive at a positive response will form an attractive and dynamic presence in the life of a congregation.

The theme of reallocating pastoral and congregational time surfaced repeatedly in the interviews. Will we as pastors and other congregational leaders be more intentional about directing time, energy and resources to the space and accompaniment needed to answer these questions about participation in the circle? Will we view the wide range of responses to this question as a threat or as a learning upon which we can appreciate and form a new experience of church?

Part of our work will be to demonstrate the value-addedness of engaging the faith and participating in a congregation. Still another part will involve fostering a more intentional community among those who can now envision greater depth and connection in sharing life with each other. This too may result in smaller congregations, perhaps much smaller, but comprised of people asking the most hopeful and joyful questions that our faith offers. As Rev. Chris Holmes said, "This winnowing may not be a bad thing."

Imagining the Circle in Your Congregation

1. How would you describe to someone not involved in a church the value that participating in a congregation gives you?

2. Drawing on one of Dycus's phrases, describe some moments in your congregation when you believed people brought "all of themselves" to be fully present for an important conversation or event. What prompted that level of presence and engagement that might translate to other deepening experiences of conversation, participation and relationship?

3. In what ways have your experiences in the church helped you discover who you are and awaken you to your best self? In what ways has the church hindered that process of becoming or remained indifferent to it?

4. What voices and perspectives are missing from your circle that you need to learn from and appreciate? In what ways might you invite those voices and perspectives to be part of your faith community?

5. Describe three initial steps your congregation can take to enrich and expand the experience of your congregation as an inclusive, life-giving, learning circle.

Two

"I sure hope we haven't wasted the last two years."

—Rev. Dr. David Galloway

Many of the people I interviewed live in contexts where issues and events were unfolding around the time of our conversation. For example, Rev. Bianca Howard, who serves as Associate Minister for Children and Youth at Zion Baptist Church in Marietta, Georgia, spoke to what life was like to serve an African-American congregation in Georgia in the run-up to and in the weeks following the 2020 presidential election. In Indianapolis, a member of Ellis's congregation was shot and killed by a police officer just weeks before we talked. Others dealt with similar situations, all in addition to leading congregations through a pandemic.

Rev. Dr. David Galloway is a retired Episcopal priest and organizational consultant who lives on St. Simons Island, Georgia. I interviewed Galloway while the trial for the three men charged with killing Ahmaud Arbery was taking place in nearby Brunswick, Georgia, which is the county seat town for St. Simons Island and other communities. A strong clergy presence gathered daily at the Brunswick courthouse to support families, encourage calm and pray for a fair trial. The jury returned multiple guilty verdicts a couple of weeks after this interview.

Against that horrid backdrop, Galloway discussed what he described as a longstanding, frustrating challenge that the pandemic highlighted again. "The church has never learned the value of disruption. We've never understood how it creates opportunities. I sure hope we haven't wasted the last two years."

Galloway noted that the world of business knows that disruption drives change, but the church values homeostasis, sometimes more than anything else. Congregations often place a nearly ultimate value on a tranquil, conflict-free experience, often because they believe conflict is unchristian and that the only tool at their disposal is niceness. They typically take a very dim view of disruption. As a result, conversations about growth often do not gain traction. Discussions that seek to assess congregational impact struggle to find a starting point. And efforts to propose change in the midst of tranquility often come packaged in meekness and tentativeness because others lie in wait to veto and quash the proposals. All of this contributes to the church being, as Holmes put it, "among the least accountable organizations in the world."

The disruption created by the tragic COVID virus presented a gift to the church. The question is, Can we view the disruption as a gift? Not the virus, not the death and suffering, but the disruption itself. This disruption created deep reflection spaces and a laboratory-like environment for experiments, learning and innovation. Can we view this disruption—and the future disruptions we will experience—as a gift that allows us to turn off the congregational auto-pilot and take a fresh look at what we do as the church and why we do it?

Unfortunately—even tragically in many cases—the disruption also shone a light on our capacity to look away from things we do not want to acknowledge and to operate rather happily in a theater of denial. We're good at protecting ourselves from things that threaten our tranquility. What if we worked as furiously and feverishly at creating positively impactful ministries as we do to quash any threat of change and disruption? The energy we spend on protecting ourselves from such things may be greater than the energy we would spend on creatively and honestly engaging those same realities.

For example, if you live in a small town impacted by population and socioeconomic shifts, the disruption of the pandemic heaped anger upon anger and grief upon grief. It has exposed our human finitude in all its unwelcome ways. Will those emotions get channeled into constructive consideration of how the church can be a life-giving presence in the community or turned inward toward a low-grade depression and what Rev. Ron Nunez calls "an ugly disgruntledness?" The same question can be asked of an urban congregation in an area plagued by gun violence and in a suburban congregation struggling to find its voice amid the sometimes bland and uninspiring expressions of faith. How will we respond to the disruption?

Galloway asked, "What will we do with this disorienting gift?" Will we use it to refocus the church toward a hurting world? Or will we continue to cling to what we have always done and wait out this disruption for however long it takes and then resume a normal that may not have been all that enlivening before?

For Galloway, one place to start is calling forth pastors who can serve both as resident theologians and entrepreneurial leaders. He says the seminaries and the churches always assess the former through coursework and ordination exams. What if seminaries and churches began assessing and valuing candidates for their capacity and willingness to be agents of change and facilitators of gospel-informed adventures?

Galloway shared a story from Christ Church Frederica to illustrate this attractive combination of resident theologian and entrepreneurial leader. The history of this parish on St. Simons Island includes the presence and leadership of John and Charles Wesley in the middle part of the eighteenth century. The current rector, the Very Rev. Tom Purdy, created an experiential All Saints Day observance at this very traditional Episcopal congregation in November 2020, a time when they had suspended in-person services in the sanctuary.

Purdy and other staff members invited the congregation to meet at the entrance to the church's cemetery where they would check-in and receive instructions. From there, people participated in a candlelit walking tour for All Saints Day. The path took people by various graves that featured a picture and other artifacts of those buried at the gravesites. It was a new way of entering into that annual time of remembrance and it occurred at a time when people were hungry for that kind of connection and reflection. Not only did Christ Church Frederica see the disruption as an opportunity for traditioned innovation,[1] they did not try to recreate the whole, usual All Saints Day service in another setting. Instead, they brought a much loved tradition into an uncertain moment through a different and welcome form.

"It taught us not to lean on what we already know."

The most surprising headline from all of this may simply be, "The church can learn!" We knew before that learning happens in the church, like at Bible studies, during mission trips and at youth group events, but in the time of COVID we saw many congregations participate in organizational learning. The initial shutdown and the subsequent waves of isolation caused congregations to face difficult scenarios and complex questions they had not confronted before. Congregations that leaned into those scenarios and questions inevitably learned new approaches and cast a discerning light on old approaches, both of which served them well during the pandemic and will engender confidence for future rounds of challenges.

So what key learnings emerged during the time of COVID? First, we learned things about ourselves. As Rev. Dr. Aleze Fulbright put it, "We learned we don't need twelve meetings to decide a matter and finally act on it. We made good decisions in the early weeks of the pandemic that served us well and we made them thoughtfully yet quickly." Her comment captures the flexibility that we demonstrated through highly uncertain days. We surprised ourselves. Now the challenge will be to weave that decisiveness and

---

1. See Hogue and Jones, *Navigating the Future.*

adaptability into a growing faith and a clear mission and not view it only as an emergency response for an unprecedented time.

We also learned that grace and trust can carry us while other things get addressed and resolved. Rev. Mindy Mayes described how she and her congregation extended grace to each other on days when the technology just would not work. Especially in the early days of the pandemic, people showed patience with the technology as long as their pastors demonstrated a commitment to stay in touch with their parishioners.

Quaker pastor Ben Snyder believes a fairly high trust was in place at his congregation going into the pandemic, which made numerous building updates possible when the congregation was out of the building for extended periods of time. I think Snyder likely boosted that trust by always asking Zoom meeting participants, "Who is not here?" and "What do I not know about this situation?" Those questions prompted the congregants to step up and exercise their leadership and oversight gifts, especially in the area of communication and connection.

These learning experiences also played out in the area of personal growth. Howard reflected on how the pandemic reminded us "that we are not on God's timing, not in control, and have a lot to learn." She reports that her fresh awareness of that reality served as a jolt to her own stagnation and highlighted issues for the church to address, especially around communication and marketing. "All this brought new life to me and to the congregation that wouldn't have come otherwise," Howard said. They discerned that, as awful as this virus has been, the church has been given the gift of not doing things as usual and they want to make the most of that gift.

Howard continued, "We tried new things and let them go quickly when they weren't it, when they weren't what God was saying. It taught us not to lean on what we already know, but to trust the Spirit and stay in prayer. Don't sit in the failure, keep moving. We tried to stay on our toes and on our knees all the time." That may prove to be physically difficult, but it's exactly the spiritual posture we seek. She also said, "God has been here before. What do you want us to learn from this, Lord? Will we be on the side of history we can be proud of?"

We also learned about our own faith traditions. The shutdown of public worship spaces did not land equally among Christian communities. For example, when my spouse and I could no longer attend worship in person at our Disciples of Christ congregation, we tuned in online, prepared communion at home and shared in the sacred meal when it came to that time of the service. However, Father Jim Sichko reminds us that the impact on the sacramental life of other traditions was significant. Sichko, a Papal Missionary of Mercy, noted that people went for months without communion in many cases. Father Joel Weir, an Orthodox priest in Crawfordsville, Indiana, took communion to people in their homes for several weeks during the pandemic.

Whitworth, an Episcopal priest, learned about a concept from her own tradition known as "spiritual communion." The full rite of spiritual communion does not appear in the 1979 Book of Common Prayer, but has been included in previous editions, most notably in prayer books prepared for those serving in the armed forces who may not have access to the bread and wine. In spiritual communion, the memory and meditation upon Christ's death serves in place of the external rite of eating and drinking of the Eucharist. The prayer book describes it this way: "If a person desires to receive the Sacrament, but, by reason of extreme sickness or physical disability, is unable to eat and drink the Bread and Wine, the Celebrant is to assure that person that all the benefits of Communion are received, even though the Sacrament is not received with the mouth."[2]

These are just a few examples. The stage is set for ongoing learning. Another dimension of this learning is recognizing that the church needs to let go of some things. These may include some treasured practices and cherished events.

2. *Book of Common Prayer*, 457.

Two

"What are we holding on to that is keeping the church from evolving?"

Several responses to this question can be summed up with, "We need to stop being a racist, homophobic country club whose rituals are empty, whose mission is self-perpetuation, and whose values can be traced more often to a political party than to Jesus." I might have just ended this section with that one statement, but thought we would all benefit from some of the more nuanced reflections. Here are the five most frequently mentioned things the church needs to stop doing.

First, stop any model of discipleship or formation or Christian education that cannot demonstrate growth in people's faith journey and cannot exercise a high commitment to mutuality in that learning and growth. The apostle Paul said that for the word of Christ to dwell in us richly we must "teach and admonish one another."[3] In prior times, this learning may have depended on an expert sharing wisdom with seekers, but interviewees consistently pointed to an experience where everyone is understood to be teaching and learning, irrespective of roles and titles. Nothing is more basic than forming people with the mind of Christ to serve God's purposes in the world.

Second, the traditional stuff needs to go if it is not representing the faith well, not connecting with people now, and cannot be translated into a form that resonates. Stale, dated traditions that are preserved only in consideration of the feelings of an individual person or family within a congregation create a barrier to the congregation remaining current and attracting new people. The above story about All Saints Day at Christ Church Frederica features an old tradition in a new form. If no new form exists or, worse, an old form is injurious and demeaning, the tradition does not re-present Jesus to the world. On the other hand, if a tradition resonates, either in its established form or in a new form, we may be surprised by who is attracted by its timely and fresh word.

3. Col 3:16.

29

Third, we need to stop being dishonest about our inconsistencies. We will lose what little credibility the church has left if our values and our actions do not begin to match in clear and simple ways. As filmmaker and theologian Cassidy Hall put, "It's about navigating love and showing compassion to each other on a personal level that makes the witness. Got to start there and maybe end there." If either our explicit language, or a particular practice, or our silence sends a different message, we are not communicating the heart of the gospel. People outside the church will pick up quickly on the discrepancies and find little reason to listen further. On the other hand, if a congregation is confessing a collective sin in which it has participated and committing to a new direction, the broader community will at least recognize our attempts at being truthful and authentic.

Fourth, over three-fourths of the interviewees stated that we need to stop missing opportunities. As a few put it, "we are nearly out of opportunities at this point!" Specifically, stop wasting time, energy and resources on foolishness in the church. It not only makes us look out of touch, it also highlights our privilege. Who else can sit around rehashing and relitigating actions from years and decades ago, all the while keeping each other's happiness foremost in their minds? Meanwhile, other children of God live in food deserts, endure housing insecurity, experience abuse and fight an unresponsive system. On the other hand, congregations that look out with eyes for the current moment and hear in the circumstances around them their calling to come alongside their neighbors in hopeful and healing ways will find new opportunities awaiting them.

Fifth, we need to stop talking about some things, or at least stop talking only about these things, if we cannot lift the discourse to a mature, faithful and relational level. After our interview, Snyder sent me a quote from Walter Brueggemann, which says we need to stop obsessing only about "pelvic theology" if all we can do is talk about genitalia and orientation and cannot move to "the relational matter of mutual fidelity."[4] This is just one example. Others

4. Brueggemann, *Materiality as Resistance*, 37–38.

30

exist that reveal how few spaces the church intentionally commits
to cultivating depth of thought and faith. As a result, candidates
and commentators jam wedge issues into an already toxic environment, cultivating suspicion at the slightest thought of complex
matters and breeding simple answers that do not honor seekers
and correspond to their questions. Hall said she is "still struck by
the amount of certitude that we carry. What are we holding on
to that is keeping the church from evolving?" And so we ask and
explore, what might nurture adventure in our congregations if we
spent more time correlating our faith to the contemporary challenges and possibilities and less time with building maintenance
and church yard sales?

"We need a lot more critical reflection with empathy."

I asked each interviewee, "How can we hold open the conversations of these two years and sustain the learning from this time?"
Their responses largely fall into these three areas.

First, find ways to tap into the passion and urgency that surfaced especially during the first several months of the pandemic.
I recognize that the virus filled those months to the brim with
anxiety and uncertainty, but remarkably, many congregations
came alive at a time when their buildings were closed to in-person
events. When I say "came alive," I am describing how congregations came to a fresh and, in many cases, a new realization of what
they value and then demonstrated a nearly unheard of urgency
about those values. This is particularly encouraging news for those
churches whose privileged social location has often muted their
Christian identity and mission and whose theology has not included any sense of urgency about the pain of the world.

People come to faith communities looking for meaning in
their lives, for authentic community and for the chance to participate in efforts that bring hope and healing to their neighbors.
When they see signs that those interests will be understood and
honored, then they may assume some of the nuts and bolts re-
sponsibilities of a church's organizational life. In 2020, congregants

experienced an awakening about their own faith journeys and church participation. In the absence of in-person worship and small groups, many people went to great lengths to stay connected.

In addition, some congregations expanded their commitments to the broader community, like Central Christian Church in Indianapolis, who regularly participates in protests and rallies for racial justice. In addition to their advocacy work and an array of existing outreach efforts, the congregation sought to address one of the economic dimensions of systemic racism. Estimates suggest that over forty percent of Black-owned businesses have permanently closed during the pandemic.[5] In an attempt to help sustain what are often cultural institutions and neighborhood anchors in communities of color, the congregation contributed $40,000 to the Indianapolis Urban League for the support of Black-owned businesses.

Second, view the messiness as the new normal and see it as an opportunity to be creative and collaborative. Caldwell-Gross, who serves as the pastor of teaching and guest experience at St. Luke's UMC in Indianapolis, says that living well with the messiness and processing it regularly will be key as congregations understand how and whether their ministries resonate with their participants and the broader community.

This will really stretch most congregations. It will be very tempting to restore old partnerships, renew prior decision-making and organizational approaches, and attempt to view religious and social issues as we did before. What many do not remember, or perhaps do not wish to remember, is that shifts in the political landscape, for instance, were already well underway before we knew anything about a coronavirus. Shifts in religiosity in the United States began impacting congregational life decades ago. It took the time of COVID for us to appreciate more fully their impact and implications.

The temptations faced by congregations who have fared well during the pandemic are as great or greater than those faced by struggling congregations who are approaching the end of their life

5. Burris, "It's Overdue."

cycle. I worry, for example, that being Zoom-savvy and technolog-ically agile will satisfy us and that we will return, perhaps eagerly, to the way we had things carefully arranged before the pandemic. If that concern proves true, we will not have pursued the pressing issues, much less challenged any systems. We will have reduced the whole season of pandemic into simple categories that present the virus as the problem and increased dexterity with technology as the solution. It will be a contemporary version of letting a good crisis go to waste.

Third, ask great questions that are, as Tapper put it, "bold, nuanced and compassionate. We need a lot more critical reflec-tion with empathy." Galloway noted that some people and profes-sions have a natural disposition toward continuous improvement. Congregations that ask great questions will intentionally seek their own continuous improvement journey from what began during the time of COVID. These questions will foster imagination and fun. They also will lead to risk and change.

This is another reminder of how misleading it is to consider the last two years as a pause from which the church can return to things like they always were. Incredible learning occurred simply by moving through this taxing time. It was not a pause if we were moving, and if we were moving we were learning. We learned about ourselves, our faith and the world, largely by asking questions.

Valuing Disruption in Your Congregation

1. Drawing on Whitworth's learning about spiritual commu-nion, describe either something new you have learned about the worship of your own faith tradition or something that you have come to appreciate and value in a new way.

2. In what ways do you believe the disruption may have de-centered some of your congregation's working assumptions (about its priorities, organizational life or building, for ex-ample) in order to free it to think about the future?

3. Describe two learnings from the disruption caused by CO-VID-19 that you might otherwise not have learned and then describe what difference those learnings will make to your congregation.

4. Describe three things that you believe your congregation needs to stop doing and why you picked those three.

5. What concrete steps will help you hold open important topics and plans that emerged during the pandemic long enough for you to act on them?

Three

"How am I part of the body of Christ?"

—REV. EVANGELINE ANDERSON-RAJKUMAR

REV. EVANGELINE ANDERSON-RAJKUMAR IS a pastor in the Evangelical Lutheran Church in America and serves two congregations in southern Indiana. She has taught in theological schools in the United States and India. In her interview, she drew consistently and deeply on themes and practices at the heart of the Christian faith, especially those related to how the church understands itself and what witness we will dare to make to the world around us.

Anderson-Rajkumar's question "How am I part of the body of Christ?" hits on several registers related to the invitation of the church to come again to the circle. Obviously, given our recent experience, part of this question explores the differences between in-person and online participation and how congregations can foster deep individual faith and a deep experience of community in both of those spaces.

This is not a new question. "How am I part of the body of Christ?" posed an important and often unanswered question long before the COVID-19 pandemic. The category of "church membership" is changing and, in many cases, fading away quickly, but that term never held the dynamic participation and accountability that would represent well a community of Jesus' followers. Belonging already looked different when the pandemic began. Any number of people who considered themselves fully committed to the congregation attended worship one to two times per month. This is a perspective that generations steeped in institutional life will struggle to understand. To add the layer of virtual participation as an authentic expression of faithfulness will be an insurmountable consideration for some.

But let's not make assumptions or rush to answer the in-person/online question when we have not adequately answered the questions about our own discipleship and our participation in the life of the church. Our pre-pandemic understanding of community need not determine our future experiences and expressions of community. Instead, let's step back from the in-person/online question. Anderson-Rajkumar zeroed in three key themes: belonging, accountability and building up the body of Christ. Reflections on these themes will shape what in-person and online communities look like rather than let presence or platform drive our understanding of the church and its values and decisions.

And when we do come to the point of sorting through the needs and possibilities of in-person and online participation, I also want to caution us against confining categories that restrict people to either one or the other. People do not identify a singular mode for other parts of their lives. In my view, a much more vital expression of Christian community will be an accountable fluidity as people participate in different groups and events in different ways.

"We belong to each other and to God."

We may participate in a congregation for years without ever reflecting on our participation. For example, do I bring positive or negative energy into the congregation? In what ways do I value and devalue others? Am I embodying an openness to the Spirit and to others in my community? Or am I seeking a blessing for my existing prejudices and my sinfully complicit associations?

What will be my investment as part of the body of Christ? This has been a nagging question among in-person communities for a long time. It will not get any easier as our communities become more dispersed. Most churches fall into one of two categories. On the one hand, many already cater to the impulses of American consumerism, allowing people to pick and choose as they will from things they like without being asked for much in return. On the other hand, especially among smaller churches, people consistently over-invest themselves in organizational machinations and their fatigue and frustration leave little room for a life-giving spiritual experience.

It may seem strange to some to start this discussion by lifting up an online community of faith. As you will see, however, what I am highlighting is the togetherness and intimacy of this particular community, not whether it is online or in-person.

I turn to Jon Mathieu to explore the question, What do we believe the experience of belonging should be in the church? Mathieu began Harbor Online Community and serves as its pastor. He also works as the Christian Century's community engagement editor. Harbor came together as a place of safety and healing for a small group of people in the Pittsburgh area. The need for safety and healing among Harbor's participants often can be traced back to wounds and losses experienced in previous church experiences. The pandemic caused Harbor to catch a larger vision and realize a new sense of calling as people from around the country connected with it during months of isolation and shutdowns.

Many congregations now stream worship services or post the videos afterwards, but do not offer much online interaction. Harbor places a central importance on community-building among the people who log on to its Thursday evening gatherings. The intentionality of those gatherings cultivates a highly participatory experience through which people "do a lot of soul-bearing and meaning-making together." You will note on Harbor's website (https://www.onlineharbor.org/distinctives) that vulnerability is listed among its distinctives. Rare is the congregation that would highlight vulnerability as a core value. At best, most Christian communities acknowledge that occasional moments of vulnerability will surface, but treat those as personal, tender and momentary episodes rather than a way of being together.

Mathieu says that the pandemic revealed "the absolute central importance of community-building to the church and to ministry. We belong to each other and to God." He lamented how other things receive higher priority, usually because we can do them in our sleep. Even theology "looks comically silly" at times, Mathieu said. Some things to which we devote our time crowd out opportunities for deeper dialogue and relationships within the congregation.

Mathieu's comments prompt the question of what witness we might have to a world bent on intentional suspicion and fracture. Whether we in the church drive the division with intentional ferocity, as is sometimes the case, or we slip into a distracted apathy, the comments of two ministers in two very different settings come to mind. Rev. Dr. Shawn Vaughn serves as pastor of Peter's Rock Church, an African-American congregation in Gary, Indiana. Rev. Dr. Hugh Hendrickson serves as pastor of Lavonia First United Methodist Church, a White congregation in northeast Georgia. They used remarkably similar words: "If the church has become non-essential, the church itself is to blame."

Harbor Church comes together online for ninety minutes each week. The gathering begins in small groups that allow the people to meet and begin to make new friends. For the next ten minutes or so, someone tells the story of their faith journey. Following that sharing, others are given the chance to ask questions of the one who shared and to make comments. This part of the gathering concludes with silence, which allows people to sit with their gratitude for the one who shared and to make connections to their own faith journeys.

Mathieu then introduces a particular biblical passage or theme in script form and participants in the Zoom gathering read parts. Mathieu, a White male, then draws on liberative biblical scholars and theologians—Feminist, Womanist, Queer, Liberation and Mujerista, for example—to appreciate the experience of other people and to bring a fresh and broader view to what may be a familiar and even stale part of scripture. Participants get divided into breakout rooms to discuss how the reading and reflections intersect with their faith journeys, commitments, doubts and questions. Each room shares in a time of contemplation before rejoining the whole group. The significance of voices other than his own stands out among those whose previous church experience minimized and excluded most voices in favor of a manipulative celebrity voice. At Harbor, the people's voices are as meaningful and essential to the experience as Mathieu's. Once back together as a whole group, Mathieu offers a closing prayer.

Mathieu says that this model cultivates a strong sense of belonging with those in each gathering and with streams and traditions of the Christian faith other than their own. A renewed, and in some cases a new, desire for belonging emerges from their engagement, curiosity and learning. This belonging is not conditioned on anything except that they belong to each other and to God.

Interestingly, it remains unclear at this writing whether Harbor will formally affiliate with a denomination or tradition. Likely possibilities appear to be the Presbyterian Church (USA) or the United Church of Christ, but the question of those bodies may be the question you are asking as you read about Harbor: Are they a church? Mathieu says, "Absolutely! I know not everyone would agree with that answer, especially some Evangelicals, but institutions need to embrace a new level of innovation, flexibility and experimentation."

"The church needs a mirror."

Dycus stated it so simply, so clearly and so bluntly. "The church needs a mirror." For the church in the U.S. to restore an honesty about itself, to bear fruit and to regain some credibility, a significant measure of our participation in the body of Christ will involve giving our congregations a fresh look and a loving critique. The church often fails to understand and appreciate how it is perceived in local communities, on social media and through its various pronouncements and activities. We lose touch with whether we are celebrating the love of God or distorting it, giving our best to the teaching of Jesus or twisting those teachings to fit priorities and prejudices we import from other sources.

All of this is true, but I know another reason why this pastorally blunt comment stayed with me. I know at first hearing that I felt a little threatened by the idea. I admit that I was worried by what a mirror might show me about my own participation and leadership in the church. A mirror might cause me to see some attitudes and loyalties that I need to set aside. It might even reveal that I enjoy some of those values, priorities and associations too much.

This is not about patting ourselves on the back, nor is it intended to push us into cowering embarrassment. We sit before the mirror as another offering of ourselves to God and God's desire for the world. Our life together will be richer and our witness to the community will be more loving and credible as a result. This is a way of putting ourselves in the Potter's hands, if you will, of seeing what God can do with our gifts and circumstances.

Dycus said, "Churches need mirrors they can trust." I followed that statement by asking who qualifies as a reliable mirror. She replied, "The best mirrors are younger adults who are actively involved in their faith communities and also operate in a more relevant reality and in more reflective spaces. Then, of course, congregational leaders must give the young adults the chance to ask questions. That's what it means to be a mirror."

Young adults, Dycus says, hunger for well-being, for a sustainable earth, for addressing *isms* that demean identities, for access to health resources, for their peers to do well, and for meaningful conversations about race, class and gender. Of course, as much privilege exists among these generations as any other, but generally "young adults do not trust institutions because they find so many of them to be oppressive and hypocritic. Just propping up institutions because prior generations found them important is not reason enough for young adults to become involved."

Dycus identifies a great approach for our needed reflection. It's possible for others to serve as our mirror as long as they can operate with some critical distance from the church they love, bring to bear other helpful perspectives on what they are seeing and hearing, and be given the access to circles of conversation and leadership where they can voice their critique.

As Dycus did in her interview, I invite you to join me in front of the mirror. Join me in centering and calming ourselves. Enter into a spirit of learning. Let's set aside, as best we can, any defensiveness that might boil up. Resist any temptation or need to explain or correct. Let's see what we will see. And let's do all this knowing that God continues to redeem and reshape the world toward hope and healing.

Here's an example that an interviewee shared with me. A congregation in a city of thirty-five thousand people was developing its congregational profile in anticipation of calling a new pastor. Someone on the church council says, "We should mention that we enjoy a good reputation in the community."

Two other people on the council spoke almost simultaneously, "Do we know that?"

The first person responded, "I think so. We all get along, don't we? No scandals. I sure haven't heard anybody say negative things."

A new person spoke up. "That doesn't answer the question. Of course we hold ourselves in high esteem." At the end of the meeting, the chairperson charged ten council members with the task of talking to people from the broader community about what they knew about this particular congregation, whether they viewed it positively or negatively, and what they based their views on. Those ten people went into shops, stores and offices, as well as talked to neighbors they had rarely spoken to before, and a few weeks later made a report to the council.

The ten council members spoke with twenty people from their city. Of that number, half of the respondents had no knowledge whatsoever of the congregation. They did not even recognize the name and knew nothing of the church's location, beliefs or work in the community. The other ten respondents split fairly evenly across a range of very positive, somewhat positive, somewhat negative and very negative. Three people expressed very similar thoughts. "A church is a church—rigid, self-serving and judgmental." This particular congregation is a welcoming, somewhat innovative community, but this exercise showed them how today's public often lumps all churches together.

This is one way a congregation can hold a mirror up to itself. The experience served as a wake-up call to the congregation and its leaders. The council stopped the search process for a new pastor and spent the next three months exploring both their findings and checking some of the other assumptions that the congregation carried about itself.

Few congregations will be eager to engage in this kind of introspection and assessment or even think it is worth their while, but a mirror does for us what we cannot do for ourselves. That can be said for most organizations, not just churches. It's why not-for-profit, educational and even corporate boards sometimes create advisory groups to observe and comment on whether the espoused values are guiding processes and decisions. Our closeness and investment make it difficult for us to catch the inconsistencies of our actions and decisions. This happens when well-intentioned but not terribly self-aware organizations operate without a mirror. As Dr. Angela Logan put it, "The church needs people who will tell us when we have spinach in our teeth."

A mirror is a small, friendly, objective group of people that can sit with us, listen, observe, ask questions and offer feedback over a period of time. That group of people will press us for our most precise responses and most honest reflections. In doing so, we will be allowed the opportunity to see our congregation in a truer light.

I hasten to add that most congregations who participate in this kind of review emerge with far more celebrations than embarrassments. In fact, most find this self-assessment to serve as a real boost as they name strengths and opportunities that have gotten buried in the uncertainty created by loss and change.

The negatives and inconsistencies will provide a clarifying perspective. Frankly—and this is not to let us off the hook for anything—some of what we will identify as negatives will be broad trends in religion and culture that are beyond our ability to reverse or even influence to any significant extent. Other negatives may simply reflect that certain activities, events and practices have come to their useful end and it's time to let them go. Perhaps we want to ritualize that ending as a way to express our gratitude for that part of our church experience and to then lay it to rest.

Still other negatives, though, call for more serious and sustained discussion and discernment. As Harber said, "We need more honesty. Get honest, get truthful about how we are doing as individuals and congregations. Stop the defaults. Stop the denial. Ask what's going on here and why." Rev. Fernando Rodriguez echoed that. "The church needs to find a way to check our norms, patterns and associations for everything we do. For example, one example is how surprised we will be just by learning what cultural assumptions we bring with us into our worship of God."

Our mirror will yield several very practical insights. For example, we will learn what we value most about life together in the church. If it's only for the sake of our own fellowship, then it does not really matter how we allocate our time and resources or how many months it takes to make the simplest decision. But if our shared vocation is to be light to the world—an empowering, uplifting, system-changing light—then how we spend our time and resources and how we focus our energy and efforts matters greatly. The first approach makes our own comfort the top priority. The second approach prioritizes the well-being of God's children and God's earth. A mirror can help us understand the difference between the two and locate our congregation on that continuum.

At the heart of this kind of reflection is the extent to which the congregation is shaped and grounded by the life, death and resurrection of Jesus Christ, by an experience of God's presence, and by our participation in what God desires for the world. A mirror will cause us to ask first, "To what degree does our congregation draw its focus, spirit and energy from Jesus?" Too often, a different question gets asked first and congregations find themselves basing their vitality on the tranquility of members, financial solvency and any notable increases or decreases in attendance and involvement. Those may show up on the church's dashboard, but all of them need to be put in the context of whether we are embracing and embodying the teaching and priorities of Jesus. Keeping a mirror handy will help with that task.

"We need to recover our own agency."

Many congregations are just too nice. Some, of course, instill fear at every turn and operate out of meanness and manipulation, but many focus so intently on each other's happiness that important and urgent conversations never get underway. This is about more than being conflict-averse, which most pastors and congregations are. This reality plays out through a willingness to let others have their long-standing fiefdoms and compartments as long as we get to continue with our own areas of control. It reeks of "conquer and divide," only in this case we are conquering ourselves! We are choosing not to look at the bigger, integrated picture and instead stay busy with some smaller aspect of church life, regardless of whether it contributes to the witness of the church or drains energy, attention and resources away from it.

It is into this all too familiar scenario that Holmes says, "We need to recover our agency." We need to set aside the notion that we are helpless in the face of the opportunity or challenge before us. This will clearly be a challenge, but the recovery of the agency for all people will be an essential answer to how we are part of the body of Christ. Without that recovery—or perhaps, claiming agency for the first time, in many instances—a passivity will continue to hang in the air for those already in the congregation and a foggy but decisive set of barriers will confront the inclusion and participation of anyone new to the congregation.

The quality and depth of life in the circle, as well as whether we take advantage of the recent disruption, depends on thoughtful and direct engagement. Thoughtful engagement refers to our care-full assessment of what about our life together truly matters and what will be truly and positively impactful. Direct engagement indicates a willingness to bring our gifts and perspectives to bear on the opportunities and challenges before the congregation. We answer the question "How am I part of the body of Christ?" with our spirit and introspection, for sure, but also with how we show up in the congregation's discernment, discussions and actions.

Most of us demonstrate capacity, access and drive in other areas of our lives. Agency surfaces when we care about things. We can exercise that kind of agency within the church and in the world on the church's behalf. But to be clear, this is not rehashing prior decisions and plans for a new cycle. The interviewees for this project talked consistently about building up the body of Christ, as the body of Christ. That is, they expressed little interest in the next set of by-law revisions, or the next building project, or the next great menu of programs and activities, unless they can be connected directly to what it means to experience God's presence and live toward God's purposes.

We can start by identifying three to four priorities and going deep in those areas to effect and measure change. For example, the mission of the Faith and Action Project at the seminary where I teach is to disrupt generational poverty and move families out of poverty. This is a focused, measurable goal. One congregation adopted a zip code with a food desert and substandard housing and committed to enhancing life through partnerships to bring safe, affordable housing and healthy, affordable food to five families each year. Again, a focused, measurable goal. Still another congregation sought to support its families' faith journeys by offering resources for spiritual practices in person and online. The pastor set a goal of fifty percent participation of the families. A focused, measurable goal. By the way, nearly two-thirds of the congregation participated.

None of these things happen accidentally or naturally. They emerge from the persistent agency of people who work through the messiness and the obstacles because they value the outcomes. Start small. Begin with two or three others. Focus your agency. Watch for positive results. Measure the outcomes. Others likely will join your efforts. Feel the momentum building in the body of Christ. Celebrate along the way. Stay focused. Enact your agency. Repeat.

Imagining Belonging and Agency

1. Describe what you hope the experience of belonging is in your congregation and then have each person compare their actual experience against that vision.

2. Develop three specific steps that will foster a greater experience of belonging in your congregation.

3. Hold up the mirror to your congregation. Keep it there for a while and hold it steady. What do you see that excites you? What do you see that alarms you?

4. Now identify the group from beyond your congregation who will look into the same mirror, invite them to do so, and set a time to hear from them what they see.

5. Who operates with a sense of agency in your congregation? What can you learn from them that will encourage the agency of others? Toward what focused and measurable good will you use your agency?

Four

"God is calling us to a more expansive faith
born of curiosity and wonder."

—Rev. Dr. Chantal McKinney

"We are more attuned to what God is inviting us to consider because of these uncertain times," said the Rev. Dr. Chantal McKinney, an Episcopal priest who founded the ministry Root Thrive Soar. The pandemic not only highlighted the inequities and suffering of our neighbors, it also created a still space for us to awaken more fully to God's presence. For months, our lives pulsed with the tension of those two realities—a pandemic causing death and disruption and a God inviting us to come again into the broadest circle of life and awareness. Even now, all that has changed are the specifics of the challenge. Perhaps the virus is reaching a controllable stage, perhaps not. Perhaps Putin's invasion of Ukraine is slowing, perhaps not. Perhaps some understanding and positive movement is occurring in the arena of racial justice, but widespread movement seems unlikely given the rhetoric and efforts to quash that progress.

The pandemic nurtured wonder and curiosity in the moments when we felt the most vulnerable. The pain experienced in the world fostered an openness among many to think afresh about what gives rise to an experience of the Holy. Is it possible and even preferred to grow in God's presence during days of delight and joy? Of course! But it's also rather easy to compartmentalize our faith from the other concerns of our lives and allow it to become stunted and stagnated. Most of us do not pursue vulnerability with any regularity. In fact, we guard against it, but our defense system suppresses joy and adventure as much as it filters out threats.

Many knew life-ravaging vulnerability before the pandemic. Others of us became acquainted with a version of real vulnerability in ways unknown to us before. McKinney reminds us that we confronted that vulnerability in our own homes. Suddenly, many spent hours in confined spaces, albeit with loved ones, when the regular pattern involved leaving the house and spending good portions of each day apart from each other. A house or apartment became not just a sanctuary to which we returned, but also the office, an all-day cafeteria, the classroom and the gym. "We had to get right with people in our own household," she said.

We did not choose this vulnerability. It was forced upon us. And yet, that vulnerability led us to ask, Where do we see the presence of God? Where is God in the midst of this crisis and how can we avail ourselves of the Spirit's comfort, strength and assurance?

This represents a significant shift from the church's emphasis on doing and on programming. A spirituality centered in Habitat for Humanity or mission trips found little outlet or expression when we could not travel or otherwise be with each other. An endless string of meetings about nothing in particular, blessedly, came to an end. So, what is left?

Ah, the Source of Life! And what followed from that recognition were moments of introspection to consider where we are finding meaning. Days of considering anew the depths of love and the heights of joy, of knowing and being known by the God who abides with us always and stirs new life among us when we least expect it. "All this revealed that we can connect with God anywhere. We already knew that on some level," McKinney says, "but I'm not sure we fully appreciated it and practiced it until this pandemic."

McKinney asks people, "How are you finding meaning these days?" In doing so, she hopes we will move beyond the narrow, predetermined and predictable paths to a more expansive faith, a faith characterized by wonder and curiosity. This applies both to us as individuals and to our congregations. She encourages us to think prayerfully about what we most want and need from our church participation before rushing back to a programmatic, activity-centered focus. "The programmatic American church has ended up looking like America—very consumeristic, always having to know how many showed up and not asking about being and belonging," McKinney said. "We also ought to pay attention to those who aren't quickly returning to church. It may not be due to COVID, but rather about valuing a life and family balance and resisting the pull of the organizational demands of meetings, projects and buildings." As Dr. Angela Logan put it, "Our church life before March 2020 was not normal. Who were we kidding? We were already in crisis with a congregational pace that was not sustainable, reasonable or humane."

McKinney invites us to enter into a season of listening first to what God is saying, to focus our spaces and energies on seeking and experiencing the Holy. This focus may lead to the mentoring and equipping for leadership and ministry that so many interviewees named, but first, it is intended to sustain our reacquaintance with the ever-enveloping grace and kindness of God and to discover the wonder and curiosity that an awareness of God's own creativity spurs in us.

The church often guards against curiosity instead of fostering it. Though it may be unintentional, people come away with the idea that the Christian faith is more like a destination than a journey, more like uncritical acceptance of precepts than an exploration of life-deepening questions. McKinney reminds us that thinking, compassionate people will not be drawn to an expression of faith where minds wither and dreams die.

Instead, an expansive faith flexes and adapts. An expansive faith trusts in God and exercises risk. An expansive faith can not only tolerate the messiness, but engage it with curiosity and see its possibilities. An expansive faith may involve duty, but it celebrates passion and calling. An expansive faith lets go of the debilitating need for everything to be perfect and finds the fun of scrappy discipleship that actually makes a positive impact. An expansive faith listens for honest, hopeful voices, knowing that insight and direction at times may come to us from people and perspectives that we have worked tirelessly to dismiss.

McKinney began to notice hawks during her daily walks. She would pause and watch them catch the wind and soar. "We can catch those currents, too. We can catch the wind and soar."

"We aren't an album generation. We're a playlist generation."

Saler's statement that serves as this section's heading describes both a cultural reality and the worship experiences during the pandemic. Not only can we tune in to worship services at our church at most any time during the week, we also can join worship services and study groups of numerous other churches.

As I write this in the early summer of 2022, many congregations are seeing a steep decline in the number of people who participate synchronously in their own congregations via Facebook Live, YouTube or another platform. This makes sense since more people feel relatively comfortable in returning to in-person worship and other activities. Interestingly, though, the number of people who view the service at some later point during the week remains quite high. This has become a way to stay connected to the congregation and to not miss the worship service.

Continuing to track these numbers and drawing on the most current set of analytics will keep opportunities before us that only a short time ago would not have occurred to most congregations. The data will provide greater understanding of this broader community and its expanded reach. Depending on the platform and what we ask of it, analytics may be able to provide information about how often individuals connect with a congregation through online worship and how long they stay online. We want to know if they are clicking rapidly through several sites and ours happens to be one of them, or if they are staying long enough to engage in a substantial part of the service. Opportunities also exist for learning more about specific ways that a congregation can support those who are worshipping by tuning in.

All of this is important and, no doubt, will develop quickly into possibilities far beyond these brief comments with the advancements of technology and with our own intentionality, but Saler's comment speaks to something more. People now have easy access to multiple congregations, their worship styles, their preaching, their beliefs and their commitments. On a given Sunday, we may worship with our own congregation in, let's say, central Iowa through Facebook Live at 10:30 a.m., but beforehand we may tune into an Anglican service from Cornwall and watch a favorite African-American preacher in Atlanta. After our service, even if for a few minutes, we might catch part of the worship from a congregation from our own denomination in Miami or join a study group in the desert of Arizona.

Who knows how long this interest may last? It may even be declining already as people settle into patterns that include at least some in-person participation. The more interesting question is, Will pastoral leaders view these varied resources as ways to live into a more expansive faith, or as threats to their tradition's identity, practices and membership? Will access to these options clarify our own beliefs and commitments and cause us to appreciate them more, or lead to an uncurated buffet of religion that may not support spiritual life in the long term?

As a pastor well before the pandemic, I often marveled at the television ministries that people supported in addition to our congregation. What would draw people involved in a liberal Disciples of Christ congregation to watch and support both local and national ministries that espoused views in direct contradiction to those of their home church? As it turns out, all kinds of reasons can account for this wide range of interests. Perhaps they were curious about the beliefs and practices of other churches. Perhaps people liked how Charles Stanley's fundamentalist preaching reduced everything to straightforward, unequivocal answers, even if those answers did not adequately appreciate the pain and complexity of human situations. Perhaps they were just curious or even bored.

The point is that even in that era there existed something like a playlist.

Now, though, we create playlists of artists, podcasts, newscasts and more. We saw the number of congregations who made their services available online grow exponentially during the pandemic. It's a new kind of playlist. Will its availability nurture an expansive faith or dilute an existing one? Will it give us many faithful paths to explore and claim or become something of a spiritual hobby that fails to cultivate serious discipleship and community?

The threats and limits of such a playlist are fairly obvious, especially without any intentional curation, but what if pastors and other congregational teachers curated these resources and kept at their disposal resources that they alone cannot adequately provide? Admittedly, I am raising a possibility for which I cannot yet provide the details or even the assurance that I would find this an acceptable approach, but throughout these interviews I heard the repeated concern that the faith formation and equipping of congregants does not receive sufficient commitment and attention. At the same time, interviewees said they did not know where the time or resources would come from that could provide the kind of opportunities needed in this area. Granberg-Michaelson said, "We've got to honor people's journey with questions at least as hard as the ones they are asking." Perhaps taking advantage of the playlist mentality is one way to do this.

In addition to the impact this might have on the faith of individuals, it also can contribute to congregational leadership. For example, Nunez talked about a theology of hospitality through diversity of worship. At Woodruff Place Baptist Church where Nunez serves, a month of worship services may include classical music with the Indianapolis Symphony Orchestra, a praise band, hip hop and southern gospel. I can imagine viewing Woodruff Place's worship services as part of a worship team's planning session and thinking through questions like: How does their worship life foster an expansive faith? What can we learn from their commitment to a diversity of worship styles? How does their approach clarify our own worship style and expose gaps and unintended meanings in our service? What from their service would be experienced as an authentic worship life and what would be seen as not fitting our identity and commitments? In this way, just the availability of the playlist could generate important reflections for the leadership and foster a more expansive faith.

"There's beauty and transcendence that I don't understand, but even in small amounts they get me through."

McKinney asks people, "Where do you feel the closest to God?" The answers vary, of course, but let's pause over the question before we begin answering it. Is this a question that you have ever thought about before? Does the question comfort or trouble you? Is this a question that regularly gets asked and reflected on at your church?

And what if the "you" in that question is plural? In other words, instead of asking an individual, what if we ask our congregation, Where do you feel closest to God? Would it lead to heartfelt testimonies or stumbling and stammering at a question that is foreign to our practice of the faith? Would this question resonate with most of your congregation or be seen as something just for "the spiritual people" to answer and discuss?

When do you feel closest to God? Many will refer to inspiring moments during worship, perhaps a line from a song, or in the silent reflection over Communion, or an uplifting, truth-telling sermon. Others will tie their closeness to the community of which they are part and talk about fellowship events and the ways we accompany one another during celebration and grief. Still others will identify occasions of serving people in need, participating in protests and joining together to effect change in their town or city.

For many, even though people re-energized their prayer lives at home during the pandemic, as Weir mentioned, closeness to God occurs in the church building. People are confronted with memories of weddings, funerals and other special occasions that occurred in sacred spaces. They made promises in those spaces, as well as said good-bye to dear ones there. I know people who come to their sanctuary each week essentially to relive prior days and revisit the times they had with now deceased loves ones. They feel close to God there.

People also feel close to God in nature—mountains and beaches and streams and fall colors and flowers and more. Soon after the pandemic began, a mother robin started building a nest on the curve of our porch's downspout. Before long, we heard the faintest sounds coming from the nest and started seeing the mother bend over into the nest with food. Then, the mother would perch on the edge of the nest and the tiny babies would stretch and position themselves against one another for the food that she brought. I was working on our porch most of the time during those months. Watching those birds come into the world and then watching them go out into the world lifted my spirits on many of those uncertain days. As unpredictable and indiscriminating as nature can be, it continues to draw people close to God.

As noted earlier, the most consistent theme through forty interviews focused on offering more spiritual growth opportunities, teaching about the diversity of ancient and contemporary spirituality, and supporting people as they engage a wide range of spiritual practices. I heard across the many traditions, contexts and beliefs a hunger for a deeper relationship with the Holy and pathways to explore and embody a deeper faith.

Some traditions and congregations already focus intently on this kind of emphasis. This is their priority. What else does the church do if it doesn't create spaces for encountering God and foster an appreciation for the spiritual life? Some congregations only do that, so their witness in the world does not serve worthwhile causes or engage oppressive systems. But some congregations don't pay much attention to the spiritual life at all, which leaves them ungrounded and under-resourced for their work in the world. "Where do you feel closest to God?" will sound like an odd question to them.

I interviewed several staff members of the Indianapolis Center for Congregations, an impactful organization with offices throughout the state of Indiana. Kate White, who served as Associate Director of Resources at the Center, made the comment that is this section's heading. "There's beauty and transcendence that I don't understand, but even in small amounts they get me through." White's reflection connects with McKinney's in important ways. Moments will occur when some experience of beauty catches us off guard. That beauty will lift our spirits, assure us that goodness remains in the world, and point us toward a dimension of life beyond ourselves. As White says, that beauty, even in small amounts, can get us through.

Commenting on what we can learn from how much most people missed being together for in-person services and activities, Granberg-Michaelson said, "It's more than we just like community, more than just wanting to be together. People are hungering for physicality in worship, that is, a sacramental life. It can't just be a bunch of words. There's a hunger for more transcendence." In other words, if Granberg-Michaelson is right, people seek more than occasional glimpses of the Divine. We seek lives—and a life together—infused with God's Spirit and lived as a sign of God's presence in the world.

Or, as McKinney phrased it, a spirituality "born of curiosity and wonder." This will involve some seeking and searching on our part, but mostly it calls for a radical openness to perceive the Holy in all moments and places.

Imagine what life-deepening experiences might come to us when we set aside our task lists, loosen our calendars, and be still in the presence of God.

Imagine what spirit-broadening encounters we may have when we relax our grip on any number of things we want to control, breathe out some of our anxiety about church attendance, organization and buildings, let go of our need to hurry or fix other people, and awaken to the enveloping grace of an ever-present God that seeks to be in life-giving relationship with us.

"We finally understand the Psalms and the range of emotions."

A more expansive faith of openness and trust leads to some mountain-top moments, adventurous journeys and animating discoveries, but it is more than just optimism and good feelings. An expansive faith speaks to all of our human experiences. We learn and grow through the whole range of those experiences—joys and sorrows, togetherness and isolation, consensus and conflict. An expansive faith means we have created a space where we can express all that we are feeling, thinking and holding.

Whitworth's comment that is this section's heading reminds us that our forebears in the faith sought an expansive faith for the vast range of their experiences and emotions and found language to express what they carried in their hearts and minds. That language, those expressions of elation and those seemingly soul-crushing phrases, may be found occasionally throughout scripture, but they are the very substance of the book of Psalms.

Within this collection of psalms, we hear of both victory in the temple and exile in Babylon. In some cases, the whole range of human experience can be found in a single psalm. For instance, Psalm 22 begins with the verse that Jesus invokes from the cross: "My God, my God, why have you forsaken me?" That first verse continues, "Why are you so far from helping me, from the words of my groaning?"[1] But a few verses later, the psalm turns to praise and thanksgiving. "I will tell of your name to my brothers and sisters; in the midst of the congregation I will praise you."[2]

The era of the pandemic, that is, the virus and all the opportunities and injustices that it created, highlighted and made worse, sent most of us into those extremes, feeling in one moment as if God had stepped away and offering praise in the next moment for someone's restored health or for safe travels or for a secure neighborhood. As Tapper said, "I don't even know yet all the losses I have experienced. I just know some opportunities, experiences and the

---

1. Ps 22:1
2. Ps 22:22

years themselves aren't coming back." Ellis offered her own lament from the African-American community: "We have been failed so many times." Dycus noted feeling publicly now what she has felt privately for a long time. Many interviewees described economic vulnerability that individuals and communities already felt prior to the pandemic. Still others spoke of decades of grief resulting from shifting population and employment patterns, especially in small towns in geographic isolation during a time of increased migration to cities and suburbs. Only an honest appraisal will allow us to move forward, but as Vaughn said, "How hard it is to hear the promises of God when we are heavy with grief."

An expansive faith helps us do that work, that healing. We must remember, though, that an expansive faith is an honest faith. Harber said, "We need to reacquaint ourselves with a hope that knows despair. Just stop pretending everything is okay and stop covering up our wounds and hurts and, instead, share our honest and vulnerable selves so we can lean into the new thing God is doing."

Yet, I know most Christians, including myself, undervalue the contribution the psalms can make to an expansive faith. We know Psalm 23 and a few phrases from other psalms, but may not be familiar with much else. I pray The Daily Office every morning, which follows the monastic practice of five psalms per day. Depending on where in the book we are, the psalms can be uplifting or torturous or, as I said above, sometimes both.

But the psalms offer us a gift made for this time. The honesty of our ancient forebears nurtures the honesty we need for an expansive faith. Our honesty toward God, each other and ourselves allows for the processing and release of what we are holding and carrying with us. Our honest expression allows us the best chance of staying spiritually and emotionally current and moving forward in our lives and in our congregations. As Weir put it, "Scripture is a series of crises all the way through. If we are comfortable, there's a problem. The comfort is not in being dominant or without conflict, but through the gift of Presence in times of challenge and uncertainty. God is here and God is faithful." The psalms, the prayer book of the church, gives us a vehicle by which to express how we are grappling and living with both the Presence and the uncertainty.

A few examples will bring to mind the honesty of the psalms. Some psalms are praise psalms, like Psalms 9, 29 and 48:

> I will give thanks to the Lord with my whole heart;
>   I will tell of all your wonderful deeds.
> I will be glad and exult in you;
>   I will sing praise to your name, O Most High.[3]
> Ascribe to the Lord, O heavenly beings,
>   ascribe to the Lord glory and strength.
> Ascribe to the Lord the glory of his name;
>   worship the Lord in holy splendor.[4]
> Great is the Lord and greatly to be praised
>   in the city of our God.
> Your name, O God, like your praise,
>   reaches to the ends of the earth.[5]

Some are psalms of confession and pardon, like Psalm 106.

> Both we and our ancestors have sinned;
>   we have committed iniquity, have done wickedly.
> Our ancestors, when they were in Egypt,
>   did not consider your wonderful works;
> they did not remember the abundance of your steadfast love,
>   but rebelled against the Most High at the Red Sea.
> Yet he saved them for his name's sake,
>   so that he might make known his mighty power.
> He rebuked the Red Sea, and it became dry;
>   he led them through the deep as through a desert.
> So he saved them from the hand of the foe,
>   and delivered them from the hand of the enemy."[6]

The psalms of lament pose the greatest challenge in understanding and the greatest hope for honesty. Consider these verses

3. Ps 9: 1–2
4. Ps 29: 1–2
5. Ps 48: 1, 10
6. Ps 106: 6, 7a, 8 and 10b.

that speak of painful circumstances and troubled relationships, including with God.

> I am weary with my moaning;
>> every night I flood my bed with tears;
>> I drench my couch with my weeping.
> My eyes waste away because of grief;
>> they grow weak because of all my foes.[7]

Psalm 31 expresses an anguish that many know, at least from time to time, if not regularly:

> Be gracious to me, O Lord, for I am in distress;
>> my eye wastes away from grief,
>> my soul and body also.
> For my life is spent with sorrow,
>> and my years with sighing;
> my strength fails because of my misery,[b]
>> and my bones waste away.
> I am the scorn of all my adversaries,
>> a horror to my neighbors,
> an object of dread to my acquaintances;
>> those who see me in the street flee from me.
> I have passed out of mind like one who is dead;
>> I have become like a broken vessel.
> For I hear the whispering of many—
>> terror all around!—
> as they scheme together against me,
>> as they plot to take my life.[8]

Psalm 42 draws together a lament about God and a relationship to others.

> I say to God, my rock,
>> "Why have you forgotten me?
> Why must I walk about mournfully
>> because the enemy oppresses me?"
> As with a deadly wound in my body,
>> my adversaries taunt me,

7. Ps 6: 6–7.
8. Ps 31: 9–13

while they say to me continually,
   "Where is your God?"[9]

No doubt, some will find these psalms to be real downers. Let's see, to what might we compare the feelings expressed in these psalms? A pandemic? Systemic racism that diminishes all of us, regardless of race? A political environment bent on self-destruction? A religious environment with leaders who fuel their ambitions with fear and hatred? The psalms may sound to some like the words of ancient people on a bad day. I hear them as praises and laments that help us pray, cleanse, grieve, and start afresh this very day with a piercing honesty.

Imagining a Faith Born of Wonder and Curiosity

1. What comes to mind when you hear the phrase "a more expansive faith?"

2. What might a more expansive faith look like in how you worship and serve the community around you?

3. In what ways would you like to see your congregation foster a more expansive faith?

4. What beauty gets you through on difficult days?

5. In three sentences each, write a psalm of praise and a psalm of lament and share them with the group.

9. Ps 42: 9–10

Five

"Going forward, we either hunker down like a fortress
to protect ourselves,
or we commit to giving life to the world."

—Rev. Dr. Wesley Granberg-Michaelson

THE PEOPLE I INTERVIEWED all captured the realities and the possibilities of the American church in different ways. Rev. Dr. Wes Granberg-Michaelson, who led the Reformed Church in America for seventeen years, noted the temptation to frame this moment in terms of time and to divide everything by pre-COVID and since-COVID. That dividing line is seductively neat and allows for conversations about recovering previous patterns, restarting prior programs and returning to normal. That seductively neat line may tamp down our anxiety and allow us to deny all that changed both pre-COVID and since-COVID, but it essentially lets us off the hook. To frame this remarkable stretch only in terms of time keeps us from valuing the disruption of the last few years and from integrating the learning of this period into the life and witness of the church.

So, Granberg-Michaelson framed the discernment in terms of the calling and character of the church, recognizing that both of these options can be found rather prominently throughout the Christian story. One option is to treat the church as a fortress, as a place where we retreat from the temptations, dangers and uncertainty of the world, and hunker down in that fortress for our own safety and protection. While he clearly hopes the church in the U.S. will not pursue this route, he acknowledged that Christians have sought separation from the world with integrity. Saint Benedict and the monastic communities that grew out of his thoughtful, intentional separation represent this option.

But what does that look like for American congregations? We are not monastic communities of work and prayer, nor are we withdrawing from the world on a permanent basis. What I believe Granberg-Michaelson points to is a posture and temperament among congregations to turn inward, stay busy with building upkeep and activities, and even if their hunkering down lasts only one hour each week, attempt to block out the kinds of conversations and situations that might bring discomfort and discord. He offered an example of how this hunkering down will highlight the disconnect and irrelevance for younger generations in our communities. Speaking of millennials in particular, "If you aren't clear on race, climate and truth, they won't take you and your congregation seriously."

So what are we supposed to do? Well, we can start by taking Granberg-Michaelson's counsel and get clear on race, climate and truth. What is your congregation's understanding of systemic racism, how does that understanding shape your congregation's commitments, and how do you express that in the broader community? Does your congregation consistently practice eco-justice or is it an adopted label that awaits your commitments? What is truth and what is true? Embarrassingly, many Christians in the U.S. are devoting their energies to lies that may prove politically advantageous, but fall short of the standard of what is true. This, Granberg-Michaelson would say, poses a particular threat as congregations hunker down in collective deceit, unable or unwilling to consider hard but liberating truths.

The second option invites us to think afresh about what it means to give life to the world. Calling on the image frequently employed by Dr. King, Granberg Michaelson injects some realism into the description: "If the arc bends toward justice, it does so haltingly and we haven't made as much progress as we wanted to believe and have often claimed." Numerous interviewees offered similarly sobering thoughts. Spells described the current moment by saying, "The tentacles of White Supremacy have come for democracy," which she followed up by saying, "Justice must be done. It won't happen apart from our action. 'Do justice,' the prophet says." We can write off our causes, end our justice efforts and fade into our community's shadows, all because injustice still exists, or we can hear the cries of the left out and left behind as a calling to engage and give life to the world.

I asked Ben Tapper, What will our faithfulness look like going forward? He said, "First, we must ask faithfulness to whom or what? Some will push for faithfulness to a doctrine or a denomination or influential people in the congregation or even a building. For me, this is about faithfulness to the marginalized. Otherwise, I'm not sure what we are doing." He urges the church to consider all we do, all we believe and all we prioritize through the lens of the impact on the most marginalized among us and the impact on creation. Part of this focus, Tapper says, will require us to undo unnecessary levels of harmful hierarchy and organization. "They tend to focus our attention on ourselves, not on the marginalized."

Many of the pastoral leaders I interviewed want to lead congregations that will give public voice to justice concerns, be an agent of healing, and show the love and will of God to the world, but most of those acknowledged they either will participate in this work with only a few interested church members or by separating from the church altogether and working toward these ends through community agencies and other partnerships. Another sobering thought, for sure, but one that reveals more communities of faith may be hunkering down than giving life to the world.

This chapter shares how three particular interviewees understand the calling to give life to the world. Numerous people with whom I spoke named some essential commitments. "It begins with showing up and showing up big," Harber said. Hendrickson reflected on how authorities at the time told the early church to stop talking about Jesus. To which Hendrickson offered a playful interpretation of those moments: "Oh, okay, sure. But have you heard about Jesus?" Ellis reminds us that some will march and some will sit at tables and negotiate and demand, and that we need more people doing both.

There's no question that we have drawn the lines of conflict more sharply or, perhaps, that we have allowed the loudest among us to draw those sharper lines of conflict, contention and conspiracy. Though the partisanship veers off into unrecognizable and incoherent splinter groups, the two major political parties continue to serve as signposts when election time rolls around. As Johnson put it, "People clearly have more allegiance to the donkey or the elephant than to the Lamb."

Nunez noted that he and the leaders of the congregation learned during the pandemic that "we could talk about difficult things." Beyond the congregation, groups act quickly to control the narrative. Caldwell-Gross said, "If you don't respond in twenty-four to seventy-two hours, you are saying what your values are and other people control the narrative." Others congregations adopt the "slow church" model where issues marinate and conversations germinate over a period of months or longer, all in an attempt to deepen the experience of community and understand more clearly what is at stake.[1] Congregations that give life to the world will find their own energized balance between proclamation, conversation and demonstration.

Specific examples can be found in various settings. Nunez's congregation seeks to focus on the neighborhood and stay in touch with neighbors with the hope of reaching teenagers before they get into violent situations. Whitworth described partnerships and alliances that help congregations incubate and launch new ministries, like Trinity Haven that "provides housing options and supportive services focusing on LGBTQ young adults who are at risk for homelessness." City Church South Bend distributed maps so that the congregation's participants could pray over dedicated

---

1. For example, Smith's *Slow Church: Cultivating Community in the Patient Way of Jesus.*

parts of their city and, later, matched several thousand dollars to support 100 Black Men of Greater South Bend.

Behind these particular efforts to give life to the world is a willingness to breathe into the pain, honor the image of God in all people and exercise riskier, edgier leadership. We turn to those commitments now.

"Breathe into the pain."

When I asked Rev. Fernando Rodriguez what image or metaphor he was finding particularly helpful, he drew on the experience of bruising his ribs in a pick-up basketball game just a few days before we talked. Rodriguez serves as Associate Presbyter for Mission for the Denver Presbytery of the PCUSA. Even on Zoom, I saw him flinch a time or two as he shifted in his chair and tried to get comfortable. He said we need to "breathe into the pain" and then shared what his doctor had made clear to him. "Make sure you keep taking deep breaths. Otherwise part of your lung will atrophy and you'll not be fully expanding your lungs. You'll be limiting your breathing. Sometimes we don't want to touch where it hurts, but you've got to breathe into the pain."

Breathe into the pain. Not breathe through the pain until it goes away, but intentionally breathe into the pain. In other words, give life to the world by making the pain of the world around us our own.

Most of us normally avoid bringing that kind of pain, complication and vulnerability into our lives. When COVID-19 began circling the earth, it confirmed our inclination to look away. Then, when the world was still and we were isolated from the widespread shutdowns, there was nowhere else to look except into the pain.

Rodriguez commented on being a Latino serving a predominantly White denomination and the disturbing difficulty of hearing people say of inequities and violence, "We never saw this before," or "We never knew this," or "We've already talked about this, it's time to move on." He said there's a remnant in our churches that's tried to remain engaged, but the structures weren't there before and aren't in place now for that engagement, so it's really hard to sustain the focus.

"How could they have not heard about and been aware of systemic racism and the gaps that exist as a result of it?" Rodriguez asked. "We've gone so long ignoring these things because of privilege that it's hard to pick this up and really do anything with it, so people are rushing back to the golden days of whatever and to the relics and artifacts that represent the comforting certainty that they crave."

We will find some of that pain in the church. Holmes urges us in a similar direction. "We are figuring out that things aren't hunky-dory, so it's painful but not bad. The church continues in an identity crisis and now is even more terribly shaken. We are going to be smaller, much smaller. Will we be okay with that? Will we really be okay with that? It will be long and hard work to come out of that crisis." Holmes urges us to acknowledge the pain, but also to see its value. We will learn from that pain if we live with it long enough and honestly enough.

We will see enormously widespread pain in the world around us. The pain into which we are breathing cannot be thought of as one event. Numerous significant and tragic events exposed in undeniable terms the pervasive inequities that plague our communities and our country. Lives are stake. Not "were" at stake, are at stake. Generational challenges riddle communities. Unresponsive systems leave people out and behind. Policies at all levels frequently privilege those who already enjoy the most benefits, comfort and security.

COVID-19 cannot be thought of as one event. Sure, it will forever be remembered and recorded as "the pandemic," but the waves of the COVID-19 virus repeatedly called for heroic responses from increasingly fatigued persons, thus dampening each attempt at community cohesion and plunging us more deeply into each stage of disillusionment. The anti-science political climate, already fueled by leaders more interested in seeing their opponents lose than in solving problems with the rest of us, kept us from reaching community cohesion with any regularity and, therefore, from drawing on that cohesion's energy and good faith.

The pain that we experienced as the church during COVID can serve us well as we move beyond this time. For example, the deep pain many felt at the disruption of not being together physically, in one space, at the same time, can lead us to critique the rabidly individualistic culture in which we live. We bring that culture with us into the church, often treating our participation in a congregation as a consumer. The inability to see each other, extend greetings, share hugs and work together on a project, all the while in a beloved space, compounded the isolation and anxiety that we experienced. To breathe into the pain of the isolation that we have known will allow us to stay connected as we process grief and look ahead. Doing grief in community with each other will require extra effort, but it is our best chance of overcoming grief's own isolating dynamic. As Della Stanley-Green put it, "The church is a place to grieve and heal in the midst of a lot of open sores."

Beyond the congregation, the people I interviewed live in very different areas from one another. I asked them, "What is or ought to be keeping the church up at night?" For some, the pain they face every day is gun violence. For others, it is poverty. Still others experience the chronic pain of battling systems that work against individuals and communities. For everyone, racism, sexism and classism diminish human life and hold back human flourishing. Every context features its own particular opportunities and challenges. Drawing on the dying words of Eric Garner in 2014, Lutheran pastor Evangeline Anderson-Rajkumar said "that the church should not be able to breathe until we are all able to breathe well."

"What does the *imago Dei* even mean anymore?"

Anderson-Rajkumar asked, "What does the *imago Dei*—being made in and bearing the image of God—even mean anymore? Anything? It concerns me greatly that it doesn't even seem to matter to the people of the church." Though this question enjoys a long history in Christian thought and in the life of the church, it arises in a particular context for this pastor. A month after she moved to the United States, Michael Brown was killed in Ferguson, Missouri. That alone, she says, held up a mirror for our society and prompted a wide range of responses and, in some cases, no response at all.

Anderson-Rajkumar spoke of a great pandemic paradox during my interview with her. "While some of us are putting masks on to guard against the virus, others of us are taking masks off that previously at least kept racist rants and actions out of public view. Those rants and actions were horribly wrong, of course, but most people knew they were wrong and so kept them behind a mask. Now, though, those masks have come off. Racism has been legitimated and encouraged at the highest level and they no longer feel a need to hide their true selves." Several interviewees of color described the pain of now feeling and experiencing publicly what they have long felt privately.

Citing the need for a new starting point in the work of social and racial justice, Anderson-Rajkumar said, "This is the first truth, our first truth. We are all made in the image of God. This is not a once-upon-a-time or an only-to-a-few situation. The *imago Dei* is for all. It's universal and it's always." But it clearly is not playing out that way. Instead, as she put it later in the interview, the racism in the church is the real pandemic. When we don't believe we are all created as equals and deserve equal opportunities, we have skewed the image of God. People wrote to her to say they didn't believe anything was wrong, even through another brutal summer of violence and death. Just as other interviews highlighted the severe disconnect between spiritual practices and the life of faith, in this case the disconnect emerged as a profoundly public one that questions a core tenet of the Christian faith. "Are we all made in the image of God or not?"

Affirming the *imago Dei* leads to a liberating effect in the world. The absence of that unequivocal affirmation provides cover for perpetuating oppression. Whether from in-person or online worship, we are sent into the world to announce good news, to be ambassadors, peacemakers, reconcilers and dealers in hope. Jesus began his ministry with a focus on setting the captives free. This is what Jesus does and this is what Jesus asks us to do. To be part of the body of Christ is to participate in these liberating acts. We give life to the world when we honor that *imago Dei* in every person.

The leadership of many congregations will seek to carve out a moderate space where, in their minds, all views are welcome and all views can be affirmed. They will stake a claim to neutrality on issues, only to reveal their confusion between being non-partisan and being neutral. Not all views can be affirmed by the life and teachings of Jesus. Nor do all alliances and associations line up with the abundant way of life that Jesus offers. The White church, especially, remains so unaware of its associations that critiquing them will be difficult. Derrer encouraged a wariness of alliances going forward, saying, "They are often about power and Jesus was wary of that kind of power. We need to be aware of that institutionally because especially in the White church the road to power often runs through other organizations. We should use power in healthy ways and not succumb to power's temptations of influence and status."

Consider the story from Acts 16 and Paul's exorcising the spirit from the young slave-girl. Her owners became very angry, saying Paul and Silas were disturbing the city. What would have happened had Paul and Silas taken a hands-off position of neutrality and non-involvement when encountering the young woman and the men who owned her? That's easy. An abusive system would have remained in place. Neutrality or silence would have sided with the slave owners and allowed the oppression and diminishment to continue on. Our neutrality does not give life to the world. Before we look away from a soul-crushing, dehumanizing situation and before we pass by without giving any notice, we must ask with whom our neutrality will cause us to side.

Though Anderson-Rajkumar knows too well what it is like to be dismissed and discredited, she is not at the point of giving up on the church. She believes that the body of Christ can be resurrected and can breathe again openly and freely and deeply, but only if it returns to a basic question about what dignity we will afford and accord to our fellow human beings. If the church itself is diminishing that dignity, what have we left to say and do? We have already hemmed ourselves into a position that we cannot sustain with any integrity. The only way out is collective repentance, but only then if we are willing to shed the scales from our eyes and see the individual tragedies and the broken systems as they truly are. She recognizes that this will be costly to the church, but encourages the church to bear the price. "The church needs to be willing to be broken for the world's sake and for its own integrity."

"We need riskier, edgier leadership from everybody."

I asked the interviewees what kinds of shifts in leadership will be needed to give life to the world. "Riskier and edgier," Holmes said, "we need riskier, edgier leadership from everybody." We are not talking about a strategic planning process here, several interviewees said, and it's more than just moving around staff positions or restructuring the organization of the congregation. Riskier and edgier refers to an energized imagination and a scrappy implementation. Riskier and edgier wades into conflict, not for the sake of destroying someone else, but to facilitate outcomes of healing within the congregation and blessing in the broader community.

Riskier and edgier commits to culture of currency, that is, addressing opportunities and challenges as they arise. Just as it did among individuals, the pandemic revealed moderate symptoms and underlying conditions in congregations with considerable age on them as a result of old issues going unaddressed and unresolved. Riskier and edgier signals a temperament to move on quickly from something that turns out not to be the approach we expected it to be. Riskier and edgier will draw on data, show up in new spaces, cultivate adventurous collaborators and focus persistently on calling forth people's gifts and passions for a new world.

In similar fashion, Derrer hopes for leadership "with a compelling vision for the life of faith because the church is part of a wider marketplace where we lose to other dazzling and well-funded options apart from the vision that following Jesus is the most meaningful life and community." A lively congregation nurtures that vision by offering a formative, orienting influence for how we live in the world as Jesus' followers, but it involves more than just inviting people to busy work, aimless events and anemic programs. As Caldwell-Gross put it, "we need to be inviting people into the life that God wants us all to have." His words echo a consistent theme from the interviews that congregations need to flip their emphasis away from heavy committee and other organizational busyness while making spiritual practices optional, to focusing primarily on cultivating spiritual depth and discernment and allowing the activities and events to be optional. In doing so, Granberg-Michaelson said we have "to build discipleship that is stronger than society's divisions."

In thinking about riskier, edgier engagement in the community, Rodriguez quoted The Message's version of John 1: "The Word became flesh and blood and moved into the neighborhood."[2] Weir, the Orthodox priest among the interviewees, asked, "Did we even care for our neighbors through this? We don't know. We plan to get to know our neighbors better and not just a one-off, perhaps worrying less about whether they come through the church door and focusing first just on just being a good neighbor in various ways."

Rev. Dr. William Smith put a sharper point on what that love can look like. "Can our presence and work in the world change the systems that cause us to have to help so many people this time of year?" He was speaking of the time around Thanksgiving and Christmas when the needs of neighbors seem to be particularly acute. Riskier, edgier leadership will lead us to look beyond the presenting need to understand what system is generating and perpetuating such wide socioeconomic gaps.

Pope Francis appointed several hundred missionaries of mercy around the world because he does not believe that the church is very good or consistent at showing mercy. One of the interviewees, Father Jim Sichko, is one of those missionaries of mercy. What would be a parallel in your congregation to the Pope's

2. John 1:14, *The Message*.

"missionaries of mercy?" What would you ask them to do in giving life to the world? To what situations would you send them?

Here's an example. One congregation chose not to write checks to its budgeted outreach causes and instead gave a committee of eight parishioners total discretion of an entire year's outreach budget. The congregation simply asked the eight to report back at the end of the year how they spent the money and what measurable impact their spending had on the well-being of people, whether that was in their local community or somewhere else in the world. They continued some of the same outreach causes that the congregation had supported for years, though at significantly reduced amounts. They spent nearly eighty percent of the monies on developing a re-entry program for women and men leaving prison. It included teaching life skills and providing support for seeking employment and housing. This ministry quickly gained interested partners. By the end of the year, the ministry was underway and had twelve persons enrolled in their re-entry support program.

And finally, riskier, edgier leadership follows up every ministry effort, regardless of whether it positively impacts the community or misses the mark, by asking the question Dycus posed: "How do churches follow moments and events that keep asking us to consider new questions and to go in new directions?" In that spirit, Rev. Courtney Armento urges us to "remember that transformation and awakening is not a one-off. If we are resisting that ongoing transformation, we are resisting the call of God into new spaces."

Imagining Your Congregation Giving Life to the World

1. In what ways does your congregation hunker down in safety and isolation from your community?

2. What does giving life—real life—to the world look like for your congregation?

3. What topics or situations—name at least one within your congregation and one in the broader community—create noticeable discomfort for your congregation? What will it look like to breathe into that pain?

4. Who are the people in your congregation and community whose divine image is either invisible, ignored or under attack? What affirming action can your congregation take on behalf of those people?

5. Identify a ministry opportunity for your congregation and describe the first three steps for launching this ministry.

Six

"Forget the fancy pieces, my people want to know my heart."

—REV. DR. WILLIAM SMITH

REV. DR. WILLIAM SMITH's interview, as with most of them, included moments of great celebration and reflections of grave concern. And as is often the case, even some of the celebrations involved sobering reminders. For example, the city of Kokomo, Indiana gave Second Missionary Baptist Church, where Smith pastors, the building that formerly housed a racially segregated school. That alone is news. A city in northcentral Indiana gave a historic African-American church a school building where none of its members—or the ancestors of its members—would have been welcome or could have ever attended. But as Smith shared the powerful, life-giving plans for that building, I was reminded afresh of the ways that the Spirit moves among us, always reclaiming human projects for good and ever luring us toward God's righteous and just world.

With Smith's leadership, the church surveyed the people of Kokomo, asking what they perceived the needs and opportunities to be for this building. The process led to creating a multi-cultural museum. Smith and the congregation have secured grants for about one-third of the projected $2.5 million project. Obviously, the museum will highlight and educate on matters of race, especially given the setting and the prior purpose of the building, but will also focus on the prejudice and violence toward Native Americans in that area. What an amazing project!

At the same time, Smith described numerous painful instances and circumstances, including his own bout with COVID and his interaction with the American healthcare system and saw up close how the pandemic revealed the depth of racism, the crisis in healthcare and the lack of coordinated community resources. He recounted several examples of parishioners not getting information they could rely on, of choosing between food and healthcare, and then choosing again quality food from very limited options. "I sat with people in some very lonely, angry and troubled moments," Smith said.

Smith's congregation entered into several serious moments of discernment. For example, they explored whether Second Missionary Baptist Church should be in relationship with the Black Lives Matter movement and, if so, what would be the shared commitments and points of divergence or separation in that relationship. Smith captured the complexity of such a relationship when he asked, "While Black Lives Matter doesn't need the church, how do we unite on a cause without being distracted by BLM particulars and technicalities? The church needs to stay true to its own commitments first."

On generating interest in making systemic change and seeing the fruits of those efforts, Smith said, "It's collaborative. The church is God's blessing to humanity and to the world. The church is a catalyst, often creating other important agencies and institutions, but we need partners. We can't do it all by ourselves and, this is important, we shouldn't. The church often gets into trouble when it tries to do everything by itself."

In the midst of this moving interview, I asked Smith what shifts in leadership style and thinking are called for now. "My people are less concerned about some of the fancy pieces. Forget the fancy pieces. They want to see my heart as a pastor and as a person." He then told me about a recent teaching moment at his church in which he shared openly about his own experiences of prayer. That intimacy of sharing further deepened the connection between pastor and congregation, between one pilgrim and a group of fellow travelers.

Hendrickson made a similar comment, saying that the people of his congregation glimpsed his humanity in new ways through the pandemic, especially when they realized his agility and care during the all-out scramble in the spring of 2020. Ellis believes that the pastor's sharing at New Beginnings caused a greater number of people to talk about the stress and grief they carried and to seek professional help for their mental and emotional well-being.

"Forget the fancy pieces," Smith said, but doing so does not come easily, particularly in the church.

"Here's a chance to learn our non-performing selves."

Matthew Barzun writes in *The Power of Giving Away Power,* "Pretending is exhausting. So it's surprising how many of us get up every day and do exactly that under the banner of 'leadership.'"[1] We know that on some level, but we probably fail to recognize how pervasive and automatic our pretending can be. What may surprise us most of all is how our roles, even or especially in the church, involve an element of pretending. This is not about being dishonest, but rather about conforming to already established scripts, roles, expectations and agendas that cover over our own identity, voices and commitments. In other words, even in our efforts toward good work and community, our true selves don't always come forward and present as we and others assume they might.

Spells named this as a major learning from the pandemic and a real growth opportunity for the church, saying, "It's stunning how much of our day-to-day movement in the world is performance, how much robotic-ness there's been to our lives that's kept us from each other and from real relationships. We need to lead with heart and without infiltration of performance and here's

---

1. Barzun, *Power of Giving Away Power,* xv.

a chance to learn our non-performing selves—just living, loving first and to fall out of love with performance.

I recognize that pretending and performing do not fully harmonize, but in this case a clear thread runs through both those words to alert us to the subordination of our true selves to various roles, relationships and projects. In too many situations, the role is pre-determined. On top of that, we likely bring our own assumptions into a given setting, which often are fueled by the expectations of others. Spells, asked, "We should always keep asking what suffices for us to stay real and vulnerable and what motivation is strong enough for that?" Only then will we escape the grasp of being over-programmed, whether others do that to us or we do it to ourselves. "Let love be genuine," Paul wrote to the Romans.[2] Our efforts may begin with the best of intentions. Our relationships may originate with the purest of motives. But whether we call it pretending or performing, they both undermine the genuineness of the love we give and receive.

As Spells said, however, something happened during the pandemic that caused us to be aware of the dimension of performance and created an opening for us to bring more of our selves forward. This is especially important with voices and perspectives that regularly get silenced and sidelined.

Some congregations realized they could come together honestly and engage in difficult conversations. Of course, most congregations offer study groups and faith formation experiences where interesting and lively discussions often surface, but only rarely do they lead to any robust participation in God's preferred future for the world. The conversations during the time of COVID pointed with fresh depth toward matters of life and death and, at least in some cases, mobilized people to be involved in ways they had not previously shown.

As badly needed conversations broke open, pastors and other congregational leaders worked to ensure they remained open long enough for discernment, creativity, learning and, hopefully, change. They understood that certain issues in the wider

2. Rom 12:9.

community had crystalized before us and demanded our engagement. As one interviewee put it, "We've never listened more closely to each other or learned more from different perspectives than during this pandemic."

Our capacity for this kind of engagement preceded the pandemic. The pandemic created an awareness. The world was still. We saw events in real time. The ensuing sense of urgency focused our attention. Now we are left to explore and decide how we will sustain our capacity for challenging conversations and how we will stay present to injustices and inequities around us.

For those still trying to break out of pre-programmed positions and conversations, Weir summed it up well. He was one of my earliest interviewees when we talked in September 2021. He described how the political environment and the pandemic had ratcheted up some of the divisions and rhetoric in the community he serves. When I asked about what comes next for him and his congregation, he replied, "We need to come back together honestly." So many subsequent interviewees echoed that prayer.

And yet, many congregations either did not attempt such conversations or were not successful in conducting them. Many expressed serious nervousness about how their congregation is dealing with the intrusion of the political climate in the church. As one person put it, "It probably means we'll never have another serious conversation about anything." That's a sad commentary, but one that already played out in many U.S. churches, often because the privileged know that squelching serious conversations is a tried and true way to maintain influence and control. It's also a proven way to weaken congregations to the point of closing.

Our culture has said repeatedly in more ways than we can count, "Forget the fancy pieces, we want to know your heart." I believe that people in the broader community first want to know of our hearts before they will listen to our beliefs or learn about our activities. When we don't know the answers to questions, the honest position is to say so. That alone can lead to a fresh round of engagement that may lead to less self-preservation and more adventurous transformation. As Dycus put it, "Sometimes our sense of knowing is used as a tool of oppression. Uncertainty and the space to ask questions undoes control and power." It also cultivates an environment where truth can be pursued, known and embraced.

"People want the truth, the hard truth."

Sichko made this comment during his interview: "People want the truth, the hard truth, and they don't trust people who make it sound easier than it is." Several interviewees made similar comments, though many of them wondered how committed people are to the truth when they are finally confronted with it. It's hard to welcome new light on something when we have worked years on an agenda supported by our carefully guarded assumptions. I wonder at times what truth I am hesitant to hear and see. Perhaps you have experienced honest moments like that as well. I know Jesus' promise. I know that the truth sets us free,[3] but I know the inconveniences and disruptions that the truth can cause before it sets us free.

Oh, how I hope Sichko is right! On too many days it feels like we have come unhinged from any truth that correlates to facts, common understandings and shared commitments. I was eating in a sandwich shop where a television had been tuned to the hearings related to the January 6, 2021 insurrection. I looked away from the television and noticed a sign over the counter: "CALORIES: tiny little creatures that live in your closet and sew your clothes a little tighter every night." The irony of seeing that sign during those hearings nearly overwhelmed me.

I would love to trust that message about calories. I wish it were true, but just because I want it to be true does not make it so. Something is not true just because we want it to be true. Insisting otherwise makes the church look increasingly irrelevant, silly and, worst of all, harmful. The church cannot challenge the culture if we are not dealing in truth.

---

3. John 8:32.

I hope we want the truth, the hard truth as Sichko called it, because for us to know our own hearts and, in turn, for the world to know our hearts, people must see our commitment to the truth. As Spells put it, "playing games is not a Jesus effort." Even on particularly self-aware days, days when I am attempting to check the honesty of my intuition and assumptions, I still know that just because something rings true for me does not mean that it is automatically or universally true. We are all conditioned by our social location, how we were parented and our emotional stability, among other things, to see truth in the things that most benefit us. We are more than capable and usually quite eager to hear what we want to hear. Things that ring true to us still need to be held up to the Light and checked out through interactions with a diverse group of people and perspectives. As Saler put it, "Whatever brokenness you see out there, look within first."

That will place us in a vulnerable position, especially in the company of fearful people who willfully deal in lies when trying to gain the upper hand on someone. The temptation will be to armor up, as Brene Brown says,[4] toward ourselves and others and deal with them only on a superficial level. But to live in the truth, with the truth, is to engage one another, across whatever lines and boundaries make us look good and others look bad. Galatians 6:2 says we fulfill the law of Christ when we bear one another's burdens. There is not a greater burden than that of only carrying part of the truth. And yet, that's the best any of us do—we all carry some piece of the truth and we count on each other to make each other aware of our blind spots, expand each other's perspectives and understandings, and fill in each other's gaps.

Do we pursue truth if it means that kind of interaction? And do we want the implications that come with truth-bearing? Brother Keith Nelson of The Society of St. John the Evangelist writes, "If you're a follower of Jesus, you're bound to be at least a little strange and a little lonely in a world bent on shaking off the weight

4. Brown, *Daring Greatly*, 292.

of truth. But however strange or lonely we feel, we remember the one in whom we are made one Body."[5]

Do we want the truth so badly that we bear the consequences of strangeness and loneliness? It's much easier to join a loud throng of people who twist facts and rewrite outcomes, all for comfort, influence and profit. We know this because most of us have done so, even if on a smaller scale and stage.

All this surfaces another question. Let's agree that people want the truth, but do they trust that the church can and will deliver the truth? That question becomes particularly timely in congregations that dare not speak the truth for fear that a few members will become unhappy and leave.

This pursuit of the truth will bring conflict and that will ask something of us that many are not used to doing. We are already tired and barely holding just the basic things together. Plus, we are worn down from conflicts all around us. To intentionally wade into conflict at this point will make summoning energy difficult, but apart from doing so, whatever we offer as the truth will not satisfy those seeking it.

Even before the pandemic we did not agree on what truth is and what is true. During the pandemic we took liberties in our construction of the truth or watered everything down so as to not offend anyone. What have we now to say to those who want the truth and will not trust any responses that make it sound easier than they already know that it is.

So what truth do we dare to speak, embrace and live by as people of faith? The discomfort created by that question reveals how hesitant we are to articulate what we understand to be true, often because we do not want to impose our truth on others and risk alienating anyone. Other congregations, however, use what they understand to be true as a means to threaten and manipulate people rather than set people free.

What do we consider to be the truth about God, about Jesus, about ourselves and about hope? Rev. Rick Spleth, who serves as Regional Minister of the Christian Church (Disciples of Christ)

5. Nelson, blog post, January 21, 2022.

in Indiana, described core beliefs of the Christian faith as land-marks.[6] It's another way of lifting up what truth is and what is true. Some traditions recite creeds from the ancient church that begin "We believe." Other traditions express their understanding of the faith through statements unique to their beliefs and com-mitments. Spleth said the landmarks include the following:

1. God created all that there is, and it is intrinsically good.

2. God's ultimate creation, humankind, tends to self-centered-ness and is thus self-destructive.

3. Throughout time God has sought fellowship and covenant relationship with us.

4. In the person of Jesus Christ, God's face and personality is revealed in the most accessible way.

5. Through the witness of Jesus we are reminded that all persons have worth and dignity and are to be treated as neighbors and friends.

6. We are beckoned out of solitude into community, away from selfishness to service.

How do these landmarks connect with the truth of your faith? What are the points of agreement? The points of divergence?

Spleth's final landmark moves from an affirmation of faith to action. We are called not just to seek what is true, but also to act on what is true. Saler asked, "To what extent must something be true before you act on it, before you love, before you engage con-structively?" To what extent must God's heart be brimming with goodness before we commit to putting goodness into the world? In what ways do we need to acknowledge and confess our self-centeredness in order to see others as whole selves and not just their worst traits? How often must God seek relationship with us before we begin to see each other as friends and neighbors?

The truth of God's compassion and justice, known to us es-pecially in Jesus of Nazareth, is intended to shape our lives to the

6. Spleth, Indiana Christian, 2.

point that we act upon that truth. A willingness to identify and work with companions along the way will encourage us to act on the truth we hold and to expand our understanding in ways that build up, inspire and focus us all.

"I just hoped we can find each other."

Tapper said, "There are lots of people out there doing really good work, I just hope we can find each other and work against these diminishing, regressive forces." Tapper's statement reminds us of the intentionality involved in knowing each other well and consistently collaborating to put goodness into the world. Jon Mathieu used the term "soul bearing." In other words, it's not just gathering in the same space for regular light conversation and like-minded fellowship, but being fully present to one another when we are in those spaces and opening ourselves to learning, mutuality and trust. Ellis expressed encouragement that more challenging occurs these days in multi-cultural spaces. When I asked her about what alliance and affiliations need to end, she responded, "It's not so much ending bad alliances as making sure truth is spoken when we are together."

When we find each other, either through new or renewed partnerships, we can understand holistic care and needs far better, build in measures of accountability, and cultivate an abiding sense of connection and community. As Tapper pointed out, though, finding each other will be challenging at a time when a good number of people are still pausing to ask, "Wait, why am I doing this? Why am I participating in a church?"

Many congregations, of course, have internal work to do on finding each other. We know names and a few details, but don't really know each other. As a result, when the political divisions seep into our congregation—though, perhaps "pour in" is a more accurate phrase—we become greatly surprised at how far apart we are from one another on pressing issues of partisanship, race, climate, conspiracy theories and more. We also become more aware of how unwilling some are to enter into and stay in the conversation.

Tapper describes well what I see in a variety of communities, both the good work and the isolation at which he points. Numerous individuals and organizations respond to emergency needs while operating from the thinnest of margins. Occasionally, they also chip away at the systems that keep people in emergency situations, as Smith described, but most weeks get spent trying to accompany and support people dealing with the latest eviction, the latest illness of a child and the latest bout with addiction, all while trying to hold off burn-out and resentment. These individuals and organizations demonstrate radical friendship with those in need, but they usually work in isolation from each other, even when they are trying to alleviate similar pain and hardship.

Tapper offered a simple model to help dismantle racism that is adapted below for building relationships and engaging in conversations about a wide range of topics. The model names ways to truly find each other, including finding each other that we may have shared a pew with for decades.

1. Begin by naming our commonalities with each other. We may assume more degrees of separation exist than actually do. We may find far more commonalties than our presumed disagreements would allow us to entertain.

2. Learn about the issues where strong disagreement remains. All issues have a history. Learn and discuss that history.

3. Discover who has been repeatedly marginalized in your local community and trace that marginalization back to its source.

4. Develop a picture that includes as many experiences and perspectives as possible. For example, if an economic system is hurting my family and me, who else is it hurting locally and globally.

5. Identify a project that you both care about and work together on it.

6. Commit to further conversations.

This is one way to find each other, to begin to appreciate our commonalities and to trust each other at a deep enough level to worship and work together to build up the body of Christ and cause our presence in the world to be a trusted one. It will not be fancy. In fact, just the opposite. It will involve a determined scrappiness and adventurous openness, but in the end we may know the truth of our hearts and one another's.

Imagine the Heart and Truth of Your Congregation

1. Drawing on Smith's congregation's work in transforming a segregated school building into a multicultural museum, is there a similar project in your community that awaits your transforming engagement?

2. In what areas of your congregation's life do you wish to move beyond performance to more honest conversations and more genuine community?

3. What is the truest thing your church says about God, about the world, about Jesus and about hope? On what do you base these statements?

4. Describe moments or issues that cause you and others in your congregation to armor up and ways to resist that temptation.

5. Who do you most need to find and who most needs to find you in order to begin a conversation that leads to a positive impact in your community?

Seven

"We need to listen for a highly contextualized ping
from the Holy Spirit."

—Rev. Chris Holmes

THIS EXPERIENCE OF INTERVIEWING leaders from around the country brought great enjoyment and fulfillment. I found it very encouraging to talk with such positive, reflective, engaged people. I hope that comes through in this book.

How these themes and experiences will play out for you and your congregation will differ from a congregation in another city and probably even from a congregation across town in your own city. "A highly contextualized ping from the Holy Spirit" will speak into this very moment, into your particular circumstances, and into your strengths and commitments. That ping will invoke the past not as an invitation to go back, but rather to draw on the wisdom of the saints and the Jesus-centered commitments of the faith for what comes next.

We will not hear that ping if we have not unlocked ourselves from previous patterns and insulated positions. We will not understand it if we are not present and appreciative of the life around us. We will not seek to interpret it apart from a willingness to honestly process our loss and embark on an adventure. And we may just try and ignore the ping if it seems to be pointing us in the direction of issues, perspectives and people that we long ago dismissed.

Congregations determined to pick life back up from early 2020 almost certainly will resume an irrelevant and insular existence that leads first to a cliff and then to a grave.

If we do not seem interested, the Spirit will continue to ping for a while, but not endlessly if we do not answer. The Spirit will not leave us. We will always know the Spirit's peace and comfort, but the Spirit has an agenda, too. She will ping elsewhere in the search for partners in healing and hope, perhaps in more receptive waters where people are willing to take up conversations like these and participate in the scrappy, fulfilling work of meaning-making, community building and human justice.

That ping is calling us to come again to the circle, yes, but more than that. The Spirit's highly contextualized ping prompts us to think anew about what life in that circle will be like and how such a community can give life and encouragement to a world straddling opportunity and weariness.

I believe the people with whom I spoke during the interviewing process are already listening to that pinging. None of them would say they have it figured out. No doubt, they wish the pinging was consistently louder and clearer, but some things they can say with confidence.

First, nothing surfaced more regularly than the need to cultivate spiritual depth through a variety of ancient and contemporary spiritual practices. Recent years raised new questions about God and new longings for experiencing God's presence. Imagine the life of a congregation that delights in its life in God. Spirituality in all its beautiful expressions becomes something we all partake of and appreciate. Prayer moves from formality into deeper spaces where we grapple with God's presence in our lives and God's dream for the world around us. A transactional faith evolves into an expansive one, causing us to reflect more freely and comfortably with others about what we cherish, who we depend on and what centers and motivates us.

Second, let's concede now, because pretending is exhausting, that the shift toward this focus will constitute such a hard turn in most congregations that it will be met with strange looks and strong resistance. As Galloway put it, "Sharing that real spiritual experience is the agenda for the church as we emerge from CO-VID. Not sure we have the proper vehicle, but that is surely the work." For most of us, our vehicle is geared toward managing church business, filling organizational slots and controlling our environment lest we be challenged by disruptive ideas and events.

We need a different vehicle in which to cultivate and sustain this more expansive faith and this deeper spiritual life. In some cases, such exploration and growth can find time and space within congregational life. In other settings, it will take root outside church structures and, in doing so, may well attract more people than it would in a congregation.

Some of our gatherings will still focus on attendance, budgets and buildings, but we will only look at those things after prayerful discernment so as to see them, and the rest of our life together, in their proper light. I am not talking about a perfunctory opening prayer. I am suggesting sustained listening with each other in community, so sustained that we are able to step back, breathe again, release pent up anxiety about the financial statement or the roof leak, hear the ping from where the Spirit wishes to take us, and then develop the specific strategies that will deepen the spiritual life of your congregation.

Third, as I imagine who the likely readers are of this book, I need to tell you that the coasting we have done on the dime of the dominant culture is over and has been for some time. Our buildings may still be adjacent to the courthouse, banks and the school district's central office, but we are not in that force field. We've been used and discarded. To be influencers at this point means entering into the fray while the most conservative community anchors work to maintain the status quo. To be agents of change, we must celebrate the positives of our local community and nation, name our sins and shortcomings, and remain close enough to a situation to help facilitate compassion and justice.

We who benefitted from riding with the culture must now speak against it when its prejudices, violence and greed get in the way of the well-being God desires for all of us. Behind every computer monitor an operating system runs in the background. If we want change, we will address the systems operating in the background, even though it will be slow and messy work.

If the fear of losing members kept us from doing the right thing before, well, that worry should be less now. We have been freed from such things by the winnowing that has taken place. Thomas Merton once spoke to this concern using the words of Christopher Dawson, "Christians stand to gain more in the long run by accepting their minority position and looking for quality rather than quantity."[1] More succinctly, Dr. King said, "The time is always right to do right."[2]

Fourth, as naïve as it sounds, we cannot abandon our signature identity of love. The words of a woman in the movie "Ferguson Rises" stay with me. "They're always showing the rage and the anger, but that's not really where protest comes from. The commitment comes from the love. Love is really the only thing that allows us to go forward."

Love fuels the imagination needed to re-engage and move forward, a love obviously found in the fellowship of the church, as well as the honest and relational love of neighbor, but most of all a love for the kind of world that God imagines even before we begin to think about it. This will be a hopeful, resilient, fierce love that will not give up on that new world. When I asked the interviewees to imagine a church beyond COVID, what I heard beneath all their reflections, stories and images is love—a love that demands an honest assessment of where we are as the church and a love already leaning into what God is inviting us to consider and participate in.

The church began by experiencing that kind of love, a love poured out in imagination.

> God declares,
>> that I will pour out my Spirit upon all flesh,
>>> and your sons and your daughters shall prophesy,
>> and your young men shall see visions,
>>> and your old men shall dream dreams.

1. Dawson, *Historic Reality*, 92–93.
2. King, Jr., "Other America."

Even upon my slaves, both men and women,
   in those days I will pour out my Spirit;
     and they shall prophesy.[3]

Acts 2 says that one way to test whether we are experiencing the Holy Spirit is whether we are dreaming. The Spirit could have blessed those early disciples with a lot of details, organization and policies, but instead gave those first Christians something else: the gift of imagining and dreaming. That's how things get started.

According to Acts, that's what an experience of the Spirit of God leads to. Men and women, young and old, listening for a highly contextualized ping from the Holy Spirit. The dreams form and the visions take shape.

What makes a church, a church? An experience of God's Spirit that leads to imagining what hope and healing in the community can look like and then going to work in intentional, concrete ways to make it a reality.

Call it a habit, if you wish. Describe it as the value-added of church participation, if that helps. But it's that dreaming and enacting that keep me coming back to the circle, again and again. It's that dreaming and enacting that caused these leaders to imagine in the midst of a pandemic's frightening grip what the experience of the church can be beyond COVID. And it's your dreaming and enacting, your authentic and expansive faith, joined with many others, that will discover the life of this sacred circle afresh and give life to the world.

3. Acts 2: 17–18.

Appendix A
Interview Questions Provided in Advance of the Interview

1. What has the era of COVID revealed to us or caused us to see more sharply?

   a. About our life of faith?

   b. About the church?

   c. About the world around us?

   d. What did you discover about the adaptability of the congregation, its currency with issues and opportunities, and how the congregation deals with conflict?

   e. What possibilities did the COVID virus allow or press the church to explore that the church might not have explored otherwise?

2. To what future is God calling us as the body of Christ?

   a. What will be the commitments of a faithful church going forward?

   b. What must the church stop doing in order to be faithful in this time?

   c. What associations, either formal or informal, stated or unstated, must the church extract itself from?

3. What witness to the world is God calling us to make?

   a. To what issues or systems in the broader community, if any, will the faithful church devote its attention, energy, resources and engagement?

   b. What is—or should be—keeping the church up at night?

   c. What is it that, if we do not address it or challenge it or live into it, we will not have responded faithfully in this time?

4. What shifts in your leadership style, temperament, and priorities will likely be needed or expected of you to guide the church in the direction of faithfulness described above?

   a. From where you find support and resources for those shifts?

   b. What will sustain the spirit of learning that characterized a good portion of the era of COVID?

5. What biblical/theological themes, stories, images or metaphors have resonated with you and/or your congregation during the era of COVID and as you think about the future?

6. Are there pastors or other religious leaders you would recommend that I approach?

Appendix B
Project Interviewees

(listed alphabetically and with information provided by the person, when possible)

Rev. Evangeline Anderson-Rajkumar, Pastor, Pastor of Gethsemane Lutheran Church and Saint Peter's Lutheran Church

Rev. Courtney Armento, Pastor of theBLEND Church Family, co- author of GA1928 and Administrator of WHOLE Disciples and Tethered1.org

Matt Burke, Director of Northeast and Education, Center for Congregations

Rev. Dr. Jevon A. Caldwell-Gross, Teaching and Online Campus Pastor, St. Luke's United Methodist Church

Rev. Brian Derrer, Lead Pastor, Christ the Savior Lutheran Church (ELCA)

Rev. Shannon Dycus, Dean of Students, Eastern Mennonite University

Rev. Dr. Alexia J. Ellis, Executive Pastor of New Beginnings Fellowship Church and Lilly Endowment Clergy Consultant

Rev. Jennifer Fisher, Co-Director of Launchpad Partners and Organizing Pastor, Imagine Cincinnati

Rev. Dr. Aleze M. Fulbright, Conference Superintendent, United Methodist Church-Indiana Annual Conference

The Rev. Canon Dr. David A. Galloway, Episcopal Diocese of Atlanta

Rev. Dr. Wesley Granberg-Michaelson, General Secretary Emeritus, Reformed Church in America

Rev. Dr. Richard L. Hamm, former General Minister and President of the Christian Church (Disciples of Christ)

Cassidy Hall, author, filmmaker, podcaster and Communications Director for the Indiana-Kentucky Conference of the United Church of Christ

Rev. Christy Jo Harber, Pastor, Woodland Christian Church

Rev. Dr. Hugh E Hendrickson, Pastor, Lavonia First United Methodist Church

Rev. Chris Holmes, Founder of Holmes Coaching Group, United Methodist Church District Superintendent (retired)

Rev. Bianca Howard, Minister of Children and Youth, Zion Baptist Church

Rev. Dr. Theodis Johnson, Pastor, Sweet Home Missionary Baptist Church

Rev. Shellie Riggs Jordan, Southeast Director, Center for Congregations

McKenzie Scott Lewis, Northwest Director, Center for Congregations

Rev. Dr. Aqueelah Ligonde, Presbyterian Church (USA)

Angela R. Logan, Ph.D., Lay Pastor, South Bend City Church and St. Andre Bessette Academic Director of the Master of Nonprofit Administration, University of Notre Dame

Jon Mathieu, founding pastor of Harbor Online Community and community engagement editor at the *Christian Century*.

Rev. Mindy L. Mayes, Senior Pastor, Bethel African Methodist Episcopal Church

The Rev. Chantal McKinney, D.Min., Episcopal priest, Missional Coach and Founder of Root Thrive Soar

Abby Miller, Associate for Resource Consulting, Center for Congregations

Rev. Ron Nunez, Lead Pastor, Woodruff Place Baptist Church

Rev. Fernando Rodriguez, Associate Presbyter for Mission, Denver Presbytery

Rob Saler, Ph.D., Director of Lilly Endowment Clergy Renewal Programs

Father Jim Sichko, Papal Missionary of Mercy, Diocese of Lexington

Rev. Dr. William J. Smith, Jr., Pastor, Second Missionary Baptist Church

Rev. Dr. Tim Shapiro, President, Center for Congregations

Ben Snyder, Pastor, Carmel Friends Church

Rev. Monique Crain Spells, Director of Christian Education/Faith Formation, Disciples Home Missions & National Convocation

Della Stanley-Green, Interim Co-Superintendent of Western Yearly Meeting of Friends Church

Ben Tapper, Associate for Resource Consulting, Center for Congregations

Rev. Dr. Shawn Vaughn, Pastor, Peter's Rock Missionary Baptist Church

Father Joel Weir, St. Stephen Church, Orthodox Church in America

Kate White, Associate Director for Resources, Center for Congregations

The Rev. Julia Whitworth, Rector, Trinity Episcopal Church

Bibliography

Barzun, Matthew. *The Power of Giving Away Power: How the Best Leaders Learn to Let Go.* New York: Optimism, 2021.

Book of Common Prayer. New York: Church Publishing Incorporated, 1979.

Brown, Brene. *Daring Greatly: How the Courage to Be Vulnerable Transforms the Way We Live, Love, Parent, and Lead.* New York: Avery, 2012.

Brueggemann, Walter. *Materiality as Resistance.* Louisville: Westminster John Knox, 2020.

Burris, Alexandria. "It's overdue: Campaign aims to boost the profile of Indy's Black-owned businesses." *The Indianapolis Star,* July 6, 2020.

Dawson, Christopher. *Historic Reality of Christian Culture: A Way to the Renewal of Human Life.* New York: Harper, 1960.

Hogue, Andrew P. and L. Gregory Jones. *Navigating the Future: Traditioned Innovation for Wilder Seas.* Nashville: Abingdon, 2021.

King, Martin Luther, Jr. "The Other America." Stanford University, April 14, 1967.

Nelson, Keith. Society of St. John the Evangelist blog post. January 21, 2022.

Smith, Christopher. *Slow Church: Cultivating Community in the Patient Way of Jesus.* Westmont, IL: IVP, 2014.

Spleth, Richard L. "In the Spirit." *The Indiana Christian* 104.1 (2022).